Living Single Successfully

Living SINGLE Successfully

HOW TO BE
YOUR OWN PERSON—
WITH OR WITHOUT A PARTNER

ROLIAND S. PARKER, Ph.D.

FRANKLIN WATTS
NEW YORK | LONDON | 1978

Library of Congress Cataloging in Publication Data

Parker, Rolland S
  Living single successfully.

  Includes index.
  1. Self-actualization (Psychology) 2. Autonomy
(Psychology) 3. Single people. I. Title.
BF637.S4P39   158'.1   78-16815
ISBN 0-531-09903-2

For JANE MORRIN
With appreciation of her wisdom and loyalty

――――――

Of all festivities, the marriage festival
appears the most unsuitable.
Calmness, humility, and silent hope
befit no ceremony more than this.
—GOETHE

Contents

Living Single Successfully

Introduction

"Rolland, I want you to teach me how to be alone!"

I was astonished by this request. Although this woman had just been divorced, both before and during her marriage she had been attractive, energetic, and full of ideas and concepts that had gained support from a variety of busy and influential people. She had worked closely with her husband. Their tie was so close that it precluded exchanges with those who could have warned them that their business was headed for disaster. Nevertheless, when failure came, they seemed to take it with good grace, and immediately set about trying to reestablish their livelihood.

Obviously, the most energetic and seemingly independent person can be frightened by the stress of emotional survival without a mate.

There are significant changes taking place in our world. Traditional Western culture is changing. Social structure, specifically the enveloping family unit, reinforced by religion, tradition, economic necessity, law, and the pressure of conformity, no longer serves the purposes of guaranteeing emotional security and social status.

Marriages occur later and seem to be fewer in number. The divorce rate is up. Conflict between the young and their elders is conspicuous. Many people choose not to pair off. Others form temporary or unconventional liaisons. It is difficult for single people to cope with their social world with anything even approaching emotional fulfillment.

The emotional consequences are serious because of the resistance to change of social imprinting systems. Family training, religious upbringing, formal educational institutions, mass media, and all the rest support the status quo. In a blind or self-serving way they pretend that nothing has happened. Young and old are bombarded with the tired stereotype that the only happy and suitable life is one shared with a spouse. As a result, many single people judge themselves to be inadequate, and their self-esteem plunges. This motivates them to form relationships that are often self-destructive and false defenses against despair.

This book faces life as it is. The single adult is frequently confronted by destructive, disoriented, exploitative, or otherwise disturbed people. It is difficult to form healthy partnerships. Mating has become like a roulettte wheel: One never knows when a lucky contact will occur. But there are ways of avoiding emotional disaster by detecting and changing destructive relationships. I encourage people to learn how to feed themselves, that is, how to live with dignity and satisfaction as individuals, with or without partners.

In this book I stress how important it is for single people to develop autonomy, but I should add that it is equally essential to the success of most marriages.

I would like to thank my friends and colleagues Lee Francis and Jane Morrin for their assistance in helping me to direct the workshops from which much of this material has evolved. My agent, Bertha Klausner, has my gratitude for her encouragement and devoted service. My editor, Carolyn Trager, made suggestions that greatly improved both the content and readability of the manuscript.

Chapter 1

The Unnecessary Conflict Between Autonomy and Relatedness

The world is full of people who feel emotionally deprived. Some are single. Others, paradoxically, are married, some with large families. The most common source of this stress is the inability to be emotionally self-sufficient. Many people have not developed their own unique identity. They have learned to complete themselves through relationships with others, looking for emotional "feeding" outside themselves rather than within. They have not recognized that autonomy is essential, whether one is alone or involved in a close relationship, that an inability to be self-sufficient either drives one's partner away or keeps one in self-destructive relationships.

There is no conflict between your being an independent, autonomous person, with a strong sense of identity, and, at the same time, being a loving and devoted mate. On the contrary, the greater your ability to enjoy your own company, the greater your capacity to form good relationships with others.

Propaganda Pro Relationships

You have been propagandized from birth that you are supposed to relate to other people. It is implied that solitary activities reflect a disturbed emotional condition. Masturbation, probably the most universal form of self-pleasure, has been called the solitary vice. Children are encouraged to play at being adults and having a family. Religion emphasizes the *sanctity* of married life and procreation. The mass media take this message, select the parts of it suitable for advertising purposes, and exaggerate the importance of certain kinds of relationships. They condition you to value yourself in terms of your contacts with others, particularly contacts of a sexual, romantic nature.

You are constantly being told, via education, religion, television, magazine advertising, and so on, that the good life evolves from an idealized kind of romantic, dependent love—which ignores the real issues of human relationships. You are encouraged to believe that emotional success depends on having a certain kind of sexual life, that emotional fulfillment follows from external, commercial additions to your life-style. What is largely neglected is the desirability and importance of autonomy. The surface image is stressed rather than the techniques of developing your ability to enjoy yourself as a separate, creative human being. The consequence is a totally unnecessary conflict between relatedness and autonomy.

From my clinical practice and human-relations workshops, I have observed that this conflict seems to be the most common source of emotional difficulties.

What Is Autonomy?

What do I mean by autonomy? Autonomy is the ability to function as an independent human being, to be effective in your own world, to experience some sense of mastery over life. It is also the ability to enjoy your own personality, to pursue and enjoy interests alone. It is the sense of yourself as a separate, worthwhile person. The autonomous person can enjoy life without constant companionship or support from others. Autonomy need not be developed at the expense of enjoying intimate, warm relationships. In fact, it is the foundation on which solid relationships can be built.

When an autonomous person mates with someone who is insecure, the dependent partner makes demands for companionship, affection, and stimulation that are draining. The autonomous party either pulls away or becomes very resentful. Clinging is self-destructive; demanding too close a relationship leads to resentment that causes the partner to create emotional distance.

It is paradoxical that dependent/demanding attitudes serve as a barrier to a relationship. It might seem that no relationship could be closer than "clutcher" and "clutchee," but the fact is that a healthy relationship recognizes the individuality of both parties. An autonomous person resents being used. A rewarding relationship permits the qualities of both parties to flourish, rather than having one party serve as a warm body.

I am not exaggerating the vulnerability experienced by the nonautonomous person. Too few people are taught that life includes all kinds of separations, that is, those caused by death, divorce, illness, anger, vacations, business trips, economic hardships, and other unavoidable events. Even in a stable relationship there will be temporary separations.

People who are not prepared to be alone often throw themselves into unsuitable or superficial relationships out of emotional emptiness.

The High Cost of Dependency

Here is an example of a marriage based in part upon a woman's lack of autonomy.

Before marriage she had two fantasies: "First, I wanted somebody to take care of me. I wanted to work with that person to make a life. I had no idea how. Second, I thought that somebody else would make the major decisions. He would be there emotionally when I needed him. He would wave the magic wand, shield me from the realities of the world. He would be my age—we'd do everything together, build a relationship, grow older together, always be together."

She had recently separated from her husband. One of her

complaints had been that there was very little sex. Recently, her husband told her that he had become involved with another woman and bragged that their sexual experience was good. In tears, she told me that she felt terrible because "My husband is a nothing, and if he is successful now, that makes me less than a nothing."

I asked her why she had stayed in such an unsatisfactory marriage for five years. Her reply was that it was better to be in an unhappy marriage than to be alone.

Men also have needs that can drive their active, autonomous wives to distraction. One husband needed his wife by his side when he returned from work. The woman was active, moderately independent, and eager to function outside their home with or without her husband. When I called her recently she reported, "I've gone back to school and I'm getting all A's. I don't worry about spelling any more. I don't feel embarrassed to have some-body edit my papers. This relieves me. I really have a talent for writing. One of my poems will be published. In fact, I feel like writing a poem about you [I was her therapist]. It's a poem about my kids and what I want from them. [She formerly lived for what they wanted from her.] I really am flying. I never had such a marvelous feeling." This freedom came after she learned that it was legitimate for her to function freely by herself. Her husband is gradually adjusting to the change in her.

Without a sense of personal identity you are likely to seek only activities that you can share with a partner. Nothing of value exists apart from the relationship. You may give up friends you had when you were single and abandon activities you once found enjoyable. Actually, you may have used all of these ac-tivities to fill time until *the* relationship came along.

Recognizing Lack of Autonomy

Let's identify the signs and causes of a lack of autonomy. If you find yourself on these pages, you can begin to develop moti-vation to overcome this disabling condition.

LOW SELF-ESTEEM: Disliking yourself can make you the prisoner of other people's opinions. Without their approval you feel worthless.

Consider the experience of this woman: "Loneliness is very hard for me. I need people. When D., who made me pregnant, called to say that he couldn't see me because he was going straight home, I called him to find out if this was true. People are like ticks that are hard to get rid of. I feel like a piece of dirt." Her feeling of being unworthy caused her to stay with a man who had mistreated her in order to get some crumbs of attention.

Another example of low self-regard is revealed by this man, an unsuccessful writer: "I wrote a great deal to please the world, specifically my family. Then I found that nobody was interested." Unfortunately, even he wasn't interested, because he was not writing for himself. His work had no compelling personal quality.

GUILT: One unhappily married woman explained: "For me, staying together is a safeguard against having an illicit love affair and being a bad woman." For this woman, freedom was intolerable because it represented a guilt-provoking sexual opportunity.

INABILITY TO BE ALONE: Feeling exposed and helpless when you are not involved in a relationship is a signal that you are overly dependent on others.

In group therapy, the members were discussing this topic. One woman said that she couldn't be alone with herself. She needed someone to hold her and occupy her time. When she was alone, she wanted to die. When in bed by herself and dozing off, she would jump up, frightened, and call her husband. At first, she didn't know why panic hit her. Then she remembered how her mother had deserted her. "She was never there when I wanted her to be. I competed with my father for my mother. They left me alone with the other children to take care of."

Some people need others around to avoid terrible feelings of isolation. It is important to be aware that not everybody who wants a relationship with you is doing it out of a tender regard for your needs. Quite the contrary. You may be the victim of somebody else's frustration and neurosis.

PROBLEMS OF COMPETENCY: Feelings of incompetence can make your life seem valueless. As one recently divorced woman said: "I'm not used to being unmarried. I'm afraid of it. I picture myself in an empty apartment without energy to take care of myself or to have a relationship." It is as though she was saying, "The world has abandoned me. Nobody is interested in me; I will always be alone and unable to do anything about it. There is no one out there who will rescue me. Poor me."

Fear of competency can also be a problem. One significant example is the self-destructive attitude many women have toward a business or professional career. They believe that their success will drive others away—men out of fear and women out of jealousy. They see their own success, talent, and independence as detrimental to their chances of forming satisfactory sexual and social relationships.

There is no easy solution. Some people do wish to dominate, or in other ways are driven to overcome feelings of inadequacy, and their methods are not always obvious. You have to assess a developing relationship carefully and realistically to be certain it is based on constructive attitudes toward you. And, of course, you must decide whether any alternative to self-development is acceptable.

Many successful professional and business women have family lives. I don't know whether they are more or less happy than women who have chosen to be homemakers. I believe that they have fewer fights with their children than those mothers who feel tied down by their children but at the same time see them as their only responsibility and source of pride.

PROBLEMS OF DEPENDENCY: Do you feel you can't function alone? Perhaps you believe you can only offer something of value to a partner, provided that he or she gives direction, rewards, or emotional support. This is a way of downgrading your own emotional resources and intelligence.

A constant sense of disappointment is a kind of dependency. Do you often feel that you are entitled to something you never seem to get? Do you still hope, despite all evidence to the contrary, that Santa Claus is out there desperately trying to find you after all these years? Do you still remember your disappointment when you discovered that chocolate Easter bunnies were hollow? Well, pull yourself together and realize that *what you don't do for yourself might not get done.*

LACK OF IDENTITY: If you do not know who are you, it is impossible to set a direction for yourself.

I suggested to a woman that she thought of herself as a figment of somebody else's imagination. She replied, "Sometimes when I make love I imagine two other people in erotic situations." She did function well on her job. There she had a role and could give other people orders. However, with members of her family, she felt pulled in all directions. "What I give is never enough. I have to equalize what I give to all of them. My image of myself? Do I exist, feel, and live in the minds of others, or for myself as well?" During the course of therapy, she said: "For the first time I became totally aware, more expressive and defined. My feelings then became more important than what other people said or thought. My own being wasn't so abstract. Now I know how little I asked for myself and what I really wanted." After a severe illness, she became intensely involved in creative art, and said: "I feel egotistic, happy, excited. I have done something fine. I'm moved by it. It's mine!"

UNDEVELOPED INTERESTS: Are you one of those people who has never pursued special interests and activities out of fear of failure? Have you sought companionship as a substitute for personal achievement?

Consider the example of a woman who found herself attached to a man who was so destructive and clutching that he tried to poison her when she finally decided to leave him. And even after she discovered that a neighbor's child had become ill from the poison intended for her, she returned to him. She felt that to be alone "was the worst punishment." She said, "I cannot spend my free time happily." She always felt on the fringes of the human race and was envious of family members and friends who were devoted to their jobs and other outside interests as well as to their loved ones.

Another woman, when she was in her late teens, told her mother that she wanted to be a nurse. Her mother replied that "members of our faith don't become nurses, they have to handle men's bodies and all that baloney." The woman, fearing her mother's disapproval and uncertain about being able to achieve her goal, accepted her mother's injunction and passed along the sexist message of self-restriction to her own daughter. "My daughter reminded me that when she was small I had told her not to be too smart when she went out on dates. She remembered that I had said men wouldn't like her if she was too smart. We were raised to think that men were the important thing and we were nothing."

LOVE AS A LOSS OF AUTONOMY: Do you feel that to be in love is to lose your individuality and freedom? This attitude is echoed frequently in the following comments:

• "I hate men that I love. I yield power. I belong to the person mentally and physically. There is an abandonment of my emotions. I hate the person for having so much power. But I like being bossed around."

• "When somebody likes you better than you like yourself, it's like getting a long-term job. Your inner guts are so vulnerable."

• "Love is like being on a drug trip. I lose control. Anyone who gets too close makes me feel as if I've lost control."

• "The more attractive the woman, the more unsure I am—the more I have to lose."

• "Loving means being responsible for the other person."

• "Being loving implies a need for commitment by the other party."

• "Being loving means that I have to demonstrate being happy, gay, and affectionate. That is a burden. I mustn't let my partner be bored or tired."

In short, being loving may be experienced as a vulnerability to intolerable demands.

AUTONOMY SEEN AS ISOLATION: When you feel insecure with your partner, do you try to increase the intensity of the exchange? This is a common reaction, but it is self-destructive when the strain derives from clutching, incompatibility, or a lack of mutual interests. Trying to draw closer may be an inappropriate solution. Independence and a little distance often yield better results.

I asked one of my patients whose marriage was shaky why she was so frightened about being independent. She replied that her independence would increase the distance between herself and her husband. I came back to the question, "What is so frightening about independence?" She began to consider it more carefully: "Nothing when you think about it. It's good to be independent if it works out. It's good to be free so that you can do what you want. If it turns to separation, at least you're independent—you'll have things to do, people to talk to. Being single again, there's nothing wrong with that, either."

SUBMISSIVENESS: If you feel inferior, you may put up with bad treatment when an aggressive, exploitative partner comes along. You may be willing to pay that price to gain some *little* warmth or status. Some people accept minimal affection and hostile behavior for long periods, even a lifetime, without making active efforts to improve their lot. They endure this sort of treatment as a kind of masochistic reproach to some parental figure. "You treated me badly, and look what I turned into, a nothing, treated like garbage." The parent can be dead, far away, or indifferent, but this unhappy role is played out.

There are ways of resolving the false conflict between autonomy and relatedness. You will see that there are choices other than isolation or total dependence. The fears of being alone or of being swallowed up in a relationship can be combated by learning new social techniques and developing your individuality.

Chapter 2

Unattached:
Opportunity or Tragedy?

Unattached . . . single . . . alone!

This condition, which strikes fear into the hearts of some, is tremendously appealing to others. It can be either a fulfilling way of life and a new start, or it can foster feelings of loneliness, isolation, and desperation. Nevertheless, one thing is certain. There will be occasions in your life when you will be alone for some period of time. Will you deal with it constructively, or will it drive you berserk? Does the fear of being alone keep you in a self-destructive relationship?

Until quite recently, few people lived outside a family structure. Traveling was expensive or cumbersome. The ground rules of life were fixed. Get married (early); have children (plenty); don't fool around outside marriage (unless you were rich and discreet); and, above all, don't get divorced (unless you wanted a scandal). The rewards for living in this pressure cooker were quite explicit. You had company (even if you hated them), you knew exactly what was expected of you (conformity), and there was a home for you somewhere (parents, spouse, or children).

Today if you want to marry, you may have difficulty finding a suitable mate because social conditions are frequently uncon-ducive. The rules are changing. Sexual fidelity isn't compatible with the concept of "open marriage" and a variety of sexual experiences. Increased mobility, higher divorce rates, and smaller family units militate against secure, long-term relationships.

But did anyone ever tell you that it is legitimate to want to be alone? Were you ever advised that some people can lead better lives without children, or even that some couples are emotionally unsuited to be parents? Did anyone encourage you to develop your own autonomy so that you could fend for yourself emotionally and have rich experiences in your own company? When did someone sit down with you and tell you that if you wanted to get married, it would be better to wait until you understood your own personality so that you could pick somebody suitable for the real you? In short, by waiting, growing up, you could increase your chances for success.

Here is how one depressed middle-aged woman reacted to being alone. She came from a conventional background and was divorced several years ago after five years of a loveless marriage:

> I have nothing to hang on to, to feel secure with. I'm anxious even when I'm with people. I do feel hopeless about my state of life. My family has their own families. I don't have a sense of being needed. By the time I was thirty-seven I was always being asked, "Why isn't a nice girl like you married?" I feel guilty about not being married. I could have married earlier. I was pretty. However, my parents' marriage enslaved my mother; my father was tyrannical. At the age of five I decided that I never wanted to get married.

This unfortunate woman is an example of so many who are pressured into relationships they really don't want because they can't cope with the state of being single.

It is likely that you too were told that the only suitable way of life is married-for-life, that normal people have children—whether they are emotionally capable of taking care of them or not—and that the person who lives alone is selfish, emotionally incompetent—or worse.

This training is not only unrealistic; it works against achieving the very goal toward which it is directed, that is, establishing loving, firm relationships. It creates dependency demands, emotional incompetence, and false expectations. Furthermore, the enormous social changes that are taking place make it more difficult to fulfill this goal. To believe that all emotional fulfillment depends upon having a special person in your life prevents you from developing your uniqueness.

Being single is more than being a statistic in the latest census. The fact of being single colors every decision of any consequence that Mr. or Ms. Alone-in-Life makes—decisions concerning sex, friendship, career, relationships with family, and so on. This status influences decision making of all kinds.

The writer is old enough to remember when the entire world suffered from the Noah's Ark Syndrome. Psychoanalysts define this as the delusion that if you are not married you are inferior, a social outcast, and unworthy to associate with decent people. It comes from the scriptural reference that passports for the voyage of forty days and nights were issued only to those who had mates. People from this generation felt like freaks until some clergyman gave them permission to have sex.

A single person is a human being without a permanent mate. According to this definition, unmarried people who live together and plan together for the future don't meet the criterion. Husbands with alimony payments and Sunday visits to their children do meet our rigorous standards. A single might be a swinging young man or woman with plenty of temporary mates. Or she could be a grayish (in personality and attire) woman who was happily married, raised children, and became widowed in late middle age. The woman, conditioned to be mated, considers it a tragedy that she is alone. The swinger, on the other hand, is single by choice and considers it a bore to be mated with two kids and a house in the suburbs.

Is Marriage Out of Style?

The marriage rate is declining. In 1975, 40 percent of women aged twenty to twenty-four were single, compared with 28 percent in 1960. In 1975, 60 percent of men this age were single, compared with 53 percent in 1960. Some of these men and women have decided to postpone marriage until they have more experience and maturity. Others, discouraged by their parents' experiences, have become disillusioned with marriage and its potentials and will never marry. The single person now has the choice of many alternate life-styles. Consequently, it is no longer possible to assume that practically every unattached person you meet wishes marriage.

Sex Roles: Changing and Unchanged

The concept of sexually appropriate roles is rapidly disappearing. Until fairly recently few questioned the sex-role stereotypes of men being dominant and active and women being passive and dependent. Significant individual differences among people of both sexes were both ignored and criticized. Consequently, the man or woman who deviated from the "ideal" was made to feel peculiar. But those conditions are changing. It is no longer scandalous for women to be sexually and professionally assertive, or for men to acknowledge their nurturing instincts, although many still cling to the old feminine and macho stereotypes. Big business is one area in which attitudes remain conservative and the single person is likely to be discriminated against. For men, having a presentable spouse is considered an asset. Married men generally have higher wages and better jobs than single men.

Single women in business face considerable conflict. They are aware that it is legitimate for them to value affluence, prestige, professional advancement, responsibility, and personal development in significant careers, as men have always done. Furthermore, the expanding economy needs trained women. So what is the problem? Many of them are unwilling to take the risks and make the investment of time that the ambitious man does as a matter of course. They are partially influenced by the sex-role prejudices that imply that they will lose their femininity if they ascend the career ladder to escape from such traditionally "feminine" jobs as receptionist, nurse, teacher, secretary, and so on. And it is true that many men do prefer to have wives and girl friends who are less professionally advanced than they.

Important consequences derive from the economic emancipation of women. A woman who earns a decent living can successfully maintain a single life for as long as it suits her. She can live alone, or with a friend or a lover. She can be sexually active or passive. She can remain a social butterfly indefinitely.

The numerous women who enjoy single status have had an enormous social influence. For every woman who is deliberately unattached, there is one less partner for a man who wants a close relationship. Conversely, there are more partners for those who desire sexual adventures. This volatile atmosphere creates a chain reaction. People with vastly different needs are brought together with no easy way of finding people who match their needs. They often are not even certain of the intentions of the other party. This situation often creates an atmosphere of suspicion, defensiveness, pretense, and withdrawal.

Alternate Life-styles

However, there are advantages to be derived from this state of confusion. New alternative life-styles can evolve. Economic, religious, and social pressure toward marriage formerly limited the possibility of exploring less conventional kinds of relationships. Today, it is acceptable for unmarried men and women to live together, something unheard of a few years ago among "decent" people. The partners have the closeness they want without any legal barrier to separation should they decide to part. The commune is another alternative. Here, large numbers of people share quarters, duties, children, and (sometimes) sexual partners. There is also group marriage, in which the number of participants is more limited and the ties are more formal than in the commune, but more bonds are available than in traditional marriage. The new freedom confronting people can be either emotional opportunity or the basis for disaster.

New Sexual Attitudes

New sexual technology has contributed to social fluidity and the change of habits. It has been estimated that sexual intercourse has increased by 25 percent because of modern contraception. Legal abortions also play a role. In the old days, if the guy didn't have a handful of rubbers in his pocket he was in trouble. There was no fooling around. If you violated this wisdom, the only alternative was a month-long anxiety attack. Today, diaphragms are prescribed for young girls, contraceptive pills are taken routinely even by virgins, and in general, people tend to enter into sexual relationships more spontaneously.

The person who conforms to the old morality in the new atmosphere runs the risk of being considered peculiar or inadequate. Your preferences, morals, sense of identity, and esthetics are assailed in all directions, and the consequences are enormous. Today you can be tossed together with more people in a short time than you would have been in a lifetime just a generation ago. You are tempted or pressured in ways that are difficult to resist. Can you maintain your identity, dignity, meet your needs, gain emotional support, and form congenial relationships, or do you become battered, frustrated, emotionally needy, resentful, and desolate?

Being an unattached person in today's single scene requires skill, courage, humor, and, above all, the capacity to feed yourself for long periods of time.

Let's take a look at some of the cast of characters out there.

One single I know is a surgeon who attends his patients every day without exception while they are in the hospital. His personal life takes second place to his career and the human beings entrusted to his care. Another single is a salesman of cheap novelty items who is as attentive to the emotional needs of the women he makes love to as he is to the quality of the merchandise he sells. Some married airline pilots with irregular schedules are as single as executives who are away from home for long stretches of time. Singles!! Who the heck are you?

ALICE

When Alice was a skinny thirteen-year-old she went to camp with Mary. Although Mary was only twelve, she was assigned to a bunk with the older girls because of an administrative mix-up. Mary was from a Mediterranean family of big-breasted women, and her early, dramatic breast development severely traumatized Alice, who decided then and there that she was an inadequate female. Alice is exceptionally bright. Her mind can handle very complicated problems. Yet, she went to college only because her mother felt that when she married she should have something to think about while she mopped the floor. Now she has her degree and she has *finished her education*. Instead of taking a position with responsibility, which might require her to work irregular hours, or committing herself to some specialized course of study, she accepted a job as a secretary in a conservative, male-dominated corporation.

Here is what goes on in Alice's mind. "I've got to get married. This is the only way I will get Ma off my back. Besides, since I am a flat-chested girl [she is a size 36 but feels like a cherry tomato], I must make extra efforts to meet men. Without having lots of traffic in my life I won't stand a chance. Go to school for an M.A. to get ahead? I won't be able to go to the bars where the action is. I don't want to get trapped for sixteen weeks with the same group of drudges."

There are two endings to this story. One unhappy. The other unhappy.

Scenario I. Last Act. Alice plays dumb and soon marries a guy whose idea of intellectual attainment is remembering the batting average of three dozen players.

Scenario II. Last Act. Scene I. Alice meets Mr. Right, but she is so demanding that he commit himself to marriage that he has an anxiety attack and flees.

Scene II (after many years): Alice has remained unhappily single. Her job frustrates her, her mother torments her, and she has taken up with Jane, another malcontent. The curtain rises at a singles dance where they both reject the social approaches of fourteen men (allocated thirteen to Alice and one to Jane). As Jane mutters to Alice, "Men are rotten," the curtain falls.

Alice's mistake was placing preference for marriage over personal development, thereby jeopardizing her happiness in two areas.

MICHAEL

He came from a home in which his parents' favorite form of entertainment was quarreling. Now of marriageable age, Michael's worst fear is of repeating the tension, hostility, and general sordidness of his parents' lives. He is very reluctant to express his feelings to his women friends, for that would create a warmth that would invite emotional openness. He might find himself committed and thus end up in marriage. To him, marriage is an ugly trap. It means only the memory of his parents' struggles. When he overhears a couple quarreling he experiences anxiety. His mistake is not experiencing each relationship as something new, with a new person and with new ground rules to be worked out for mutual satisfaction.

JAMES

James came from a similar background as Michael, but he was a less vulnerable child. He learned to benefit from his parents' fights. Knowing their mutual antagonism, he manipulated one against the other. He has just one weakness. James is socially insensitive. You see, he doesn't take anger seriously. When he sees people in a violent confrontation, he doesn't recognize that they are in emotional pain. Knowing no better, he cheerfully abuses the women he dates and then is puzzled by the brief duration of his relationships.

KATHY

Kathy married when she was very young, had several children, and devoted her life to them. She and her husband, Bill, had nothing in common except the children, but they acted as devoted parents. When the children were older, Kathy and Bill went out a bit, primarily to play cards with a small circle of friends. Occasionally they would take a trip together. Kathy had no interests, no hobbies, and hadn't taken a course since high school. Unfortunately, her husband died when she was still young enough to want social and sexual activity but too old to have access to many men. Her friends no longer invite her because she is not part of a couple; her children are married and far from home. She is handicapped in mobility because she doesn't have funds for a car. Public transportation and urban conditions frighten her. She is desperate for companionship but has found only one friend, a recently widowed woman who feels even more frightened and inadequate than Kathy. She demands that Kathy constantly visit her at her house. Kathy is different from many other singles because she was forced to be alone late in life. But she is unprepared because she never developed any autonomy. There is nothing that she can do by herself that brings her any pleasure.

BEN

Ben came from a Jewish family who lived in a Jewish community. Because of poverty and the disorganization that followed the death of his father when he was five, the ceremony of confirmation at age thirteen was neglected. He did not have a Bar Mitzvah! This omission left him feeling deprived and socially inadequate. He never had the honor of making a speech in synagogue and celebrating the traditional rite of passage with family, friends, and neighbors. Ben is now forty-five and prefers to socialize with men and women of his own faith. But God forbid he should admit that thirty-two years ago he was not Bar Mitzvahed. This preoccupation with the indignity he suffered as a child causes him to disqualify himself with religious women he respects. Rather, he confines his attentions to those he considers his inferiors, and even to them, he cannot admit his feeling of humiliation.

SANDRA

Sandra was caught up in the craze for early marriage after World War II. She would have eloped when she was fourteen if she had had a boyfriend. When at the age of twenty she finally met Robert—who couldn't stand either his parents or his elder brother—she felt she was already a spinster and jumped at the opportunity to marry him. At that point she knew nothing about the direction in which her personality or her husband's would develop. By the time her two children were born the stresses in her marriage included sexual problems, irritability, and an inability to concur in major decisions. The couple was mismatched but reluctant to separate because of the consequences of divorce on their children. Eventually they split because they genuinely didn't like each other any more. Sandra, then age thirty, had custody of the children, which put a strain on her social life. The men she met did not enjoy the fatherly role that she insisted on—taking Sandra and the children to the zoo, the circus, and the movies was not what they had in mind.

The scene now changes to a social-skills workshop attended by Sandra and her friend Grace. The early experience of one participant, who was raised by foster parents, is about to be acted out. Chairs are arranged to resemble the front and rear seats of a car. Sandra plays the mother and George—a good-looking bachelor who has all the companionship he needs without getting married—plays the resentful foster father. The family is going on a picnic. The role players (foster parents, sister, and protagonist) take their places in the "car."

GEORGE: This reminds me of an experience. I used to go out with a woman with two children and their needs came first. I didn't want to go to the circus.

SANDRA: It is a great pleasure to watch young children enjoy the circus.

LEADER: George is too busy being an adult to enjoy the children.

SANDRA: I've had enough of this, did you hear him?

GRACE *(Sandra's friend):* I've got two children also.

Exeunt both Sandra and Grace from the workshop in a rage. They resent any men who can't get involved with their children.

TOM

Tom is a sales manager. Things were really tight for his parents in the years before he was born during the Depression. His family's "Depression mentality" persisted long after the financial pressures had eased. They never took vacations and thought that using taxis was sinful. Tom grew up deeply influenced by the chronic economic anxiety of his parents. Today, he works day and night. He is on the road about half of the time supervising the men in his department and creating new business. When he is in town, he stays late at the office *finding things to do.* When he requested assistance, the owner of his company (who "thinks small") didn't believe he needed any. Finally a totally unqualified switchboard operator was made his secretary. He cannot rely on her to look after his business affairs for the two-week stretches that he travels. Tom has gone from one woman to another because he is never around long enough for bonds of affection and commitment to develop.

KI-KI

Finally, there is the case of Ki-Ki (born Priscilla). Ki-Ki is a flight attendant who lives on the swinging East Side of Manhattan. She was the only girl among six children. She was the firstborn and there was always a younger brother who was in trouble, needed his face washed, or couldn't understand arithmetic. Her mother was a drudge, her father a male chauvinist. If there was work to be done around the house it was the women's responsibility. When Ki-Ki graduated from high school she left home and moved to New York where she soon became involved with a man. She lived with him despite the fact that he beat and otherwise degraded her. During this period she went to college for a while, then decided to train to be a flight attendant, and ultimately got a job with a major airline. She now shares an apartment with a couple of other young women in a new high-priced apartment building famous for its singles parties. Her schedule is irregular. She travels free or at minimal expense during all of her vacation time. Every nickel goes into clothes, vacations, and rent. She has decided that she will never marry because she can only anticipate repeating her childhood image of drudgery.

All of these people lead lives conditioned by their attitudes toward marriage and by their state of being single.

They cannot share their experiences with a mate.

They are excluded from the society of married people to a large extent.

Their social life revolves around other single people.

They fear moving to any area to live unless there are other singles.

For years they were discriminated against at tax time.

Some positions in industry· are closed to them because of prejudice against unmarried people.

They do not apply for certain positions because they are ashamed to admit during interviews that they are divorced or unmarried.

Some of them are miserably lonely.

Others swing from one relationship to another, frequently picking up emotional scars along the way.

All of them are emotionally hungry if they were to admit it.

All of them are rotten decision makers because they live in the past and permit events that are no longer relevant to affect their relationships, career, education, leisure time, and almost every other area of their lives.

We now have identified this strange condition. Can we cure it?

Chapter 3

Is Singleness Emotional Leprosy?

I wouldn't want to minimize some of the legitimate disadvantages of being single. There is no doubt that enjoying and benefiting from human companionship is built into our genes. Our ancestors were able to survive in a hostile environment by relying on each other for support against threats from predatory animals, competing humanlike creatures, and adverse weather conditions. Grouping together made dangers easier to deal with. The secrets of survival were transmitted within the family and the clan. As a consequence, those individuals who could not react in a social way were undoubtedly excluded and their genes did not contribute to our species. What was initially a matter of natural selection, or survival of the fittest, has become transformed into a social pattern.

Those of you who are not living in an intimate relationship today can be subject to considerable stress. First, you may be deprived of some basic needs. Second, you do not benefit from the structure of society, which was designed for couples. Third, you are disapproved of by those who have either a stake in the status quo or a neurotic resentment of the benefits of an alternative life-style.

Thus, the single state encourages all sorts of emotional discomfort, from the frankly neurotic to the inconvenient to being the butt of others' arrogance and hostility. You must recognize that it is largely the result of your own frame of mind and that it need not be a permanent condition. If you are willing to accept responsibility for your choice of life-style and relinquish self-destructive patterns, you are ready to enjoy life as a single or as a member of a couple. I am not promising you heaven on earth, because there are too many real hazards in the world, but you can feel like an equal and create happy opportunities and emotional fulfillment for yourself.

Why Unhappiness?

The basic reasons for single (and mismated couple) unhappiness include the following:

• *Prior Conditioning.* You feel inadequate, guilty, fearful. You assail yourself with all kinds of doubts. You constantly live in the past as though the cruelties, injustices, and unpleasant accidents of fate are destined to be repeated forever. You do not experience every situation as a new one.

Fear is the most frequent emotional complaint of the singles that I come in contact with. Here are some of the ways in which they experience it.

"I want release of anxiety; I am afraid and need people's support; I'm depressed and I stay in bed. My friends are on the same depression kick; I'm still scared shit, so I can't take risks. Telling someone to take risks doesn't help; I can't handle emotional pain. I have been wiped out by somebody I had put my faith in; I want to explore the world of people with less tension—and have more fun; I want to be at ease with people at the emotional level, not only the superficial level; I am uncomfortable and shy with strangers (or with people I know) and I make them uncomfortable; I want to be with people because I am in a kind of pain; I want to be brought out and be less inhibited; I am supersensitive and I take things to heart. I worry about things that may happen and rarely do; I get lost in a group; I am afraid to state my opinion because I might be judged, so I don't say what I really mean; I don't know why I get so anxious and make such a problem about meeting people."

What is involved is self-destructive, persistent irrational fear with a touch of hopelessness.

• *Lack of Good Models and Training.* It is extremely important that human beings learn from their parents. Other species learn basic living techniques from their parents. Unfortunately, too many humans learn just the opposite from theirs—and have to spend years unlearning self-destructive behavior. But it can be done!

Neurotic conditioning results when parents teach their children that they are immoral, unsatisfactory to their parents, inadequate when compared to their siblings and peers, and so on. Also, parents often show by example how to be cowardly. Parents' fears of particular situations increase the likelihood that their children will be fearful of the same events. As one researcher, John Bowlby, noted in his book, *Attachment,** our nervous system probably is constructed in such a way that "whenever we are in a strange or otherwise potentially dangerous situation we commonly make a point of observing how others are responding and take our cue from them."

Here are some examples by which people learn habits of fear and social estrangement: The father who permits himself to be degraded by his supervisor teaches his children that authority figures are dangerous; the mother who tells her children to behave nicely so that she won't be embarrassed before the neighbors teaches them that other people's opinions are very important; fear of other ethnic groups is a prime example of poor modeling.

• *Incorrect Conclusions About Life.* A whole group of particular misconceptions about life occur repeatedly in dissatisfied single people (and are also shared by many couples).

People have different opinions: It comes as a painful surprise

---

* John Bowlby, *Attachment,* Attachment and Loss Series, Vol. 1 (New York: Basic Books, 1969).

to many singles that their concepts about sexual pacing (when, how frequently, and with whom) are not shared by others. This lack of awareness or respect for the individuality of others results in frequent rejections. People come to their beliefs and attitudes through complex routes. There are many shades of meaning in any topic that affects human relationships. Therefore, if you consistently expect others to feel as you do about what is appropriate, you are due for a painful surprise and a quick separation. Imposing your beliefs on others keeps you from making constructive compromises, learning anything new, changing, taking risks, or exploring new situations. Admitting that others have a right to have different beliefs leaves you open to doubt—and to growth.

Stability equals security: Learning from experience means taking risks or changing your behavior in some way in order to achieve success or pleasure. Clinging to a stable but unrewarding situation only prevents you from trying potentially pleasurable activities.

It is important to be able to say, "I am unhappy or unsuccessful in some matter of great importance to me. The way I have led my life or handled this kind of affair is inefficient and self-destructive. Therefore, I must change." What didn't work yesterday is not likely to be a solution for today. What worked well today may not be as effective in a different situation tomorrow. True security comes from keeping your eyes and ears open to shifting conditions around you, to the daily changes in your own strengths, moods, and attitudes, and from recognizing the actual transactions between yourself and the world. When you do that, you are able to react appropriately to the varied people and situations you confront. You might intuitively select effective behavior. Even a trial-and-error approach offers more hope than rigid reliance on the usual way of doing things.

I like to remember what a smart rat does when a psychologist puts it in a maze, a new situation. It runs about, hits its nose in a blind alley, and then tries something new. I think that you can do at least as well as a rat.

A friend is someone who agrees with you: About the best way to continue making the same error is to surround yourself with people who echo all your opinions. Sandra and Grace are examples of that sort of self-defeating pattern. Instead of working out their problems and achieving insight into why some men have problems in relating to women with children, they supported each other's belief that such guys are no good. They left the situation without learning anything new. What happens when two friends with identical beliefs compare notes is that stereotypes become verified. By confining your circle of friends to those who are think-alikes you are merely confirming your own misconceptions.

JOE: Joan just betrayed me with Tom.
MOE: Women can't be trusted.

SALLY: Moe couldn't keep his dirty paws off me.
SARAH: That's all men are interested in.

Find a friend who has the courage to disagree with you. That is a relationship to be treasured.

Love me, love my ideas: As a person who dislikes hostile relationships, I need an honest technique for keeping out of fights. Not that I am recommending cowardice or self-effacement. However, I have discovered the secret of avoiding 75.38 percent of unnecessary fights. If you pay close attention to it, your social relationships will miraculously improve.

Most people believe that *all* ideas are important. When friends confront them with ideas that differ from theirs, they react as if those ideas were life threatening. They feel challenged and leap in to correct the "misconceptions."

Choose the areas that are really vital to your welfare. The remainder are trivial. My solution is to ignore many points of disagreement. Another way to avoid fights, and thus isolation from others, is to acknowledge the difference and then state: "I don't think that we can convince each other. I would rather talk about something else."

Friendship at all costs: There is no doubt that friendship is important. The question is, what kind of friendship? Is there any reason to maintain a relationship that is destructive to you? Remember, there is a decided difference between loyalty and self-sacrifice. You have to learn how to let go, to decide whether at a given time somebody is enhancing your life or detracting from it. After all, if married people can get divorces, single people have the same rights. You don't owe loyalty to anyone who is unsupportive or selfish or who enhances his or her ego at your expense. Get a premarital divorce!

• *Lack of Skill Training.* Many people will tell you that the road to social success is "just be yourself." No doubt it works for some individuals who have had the good fortune to grow up without the emotional scarring that makes so many of us inhibited, unnatural, and anxious in social situations. It is a cruel paradox that the only substitute for social skills is a kind of courage, and those people who are deficient in their social education are most likely to be deficient in courage as well.

If some of you feel socially awkward, it is probably because your parents ignored this part of your training. Or you may be hampered because your social skills have become outdated. If you have lost a mate after many years of marriage you may feel out of touch with the current techniques of dating and courtship, as well as with ideas concerning sexuality and relationships between the sexes.

Here a little self-appraisal is necessary. Are you out of date? Are there aspects of social behavior that you simply don't know or understand? Constant rejections, the sense that others are uncomfortable with you, or the feeling that you are out of place in ordinary social situations suggest that your social skills need some polishing. A trusted, socially adept friend can be a great help. When in doubt ask that friend for advice on what is appropriate in the various social situations that interest you. You will soon find that your own growing self-awareness serves as a reliable guide. Remember, too, that understanding how others react does not mean that you have to acquiesce to their needs. It simply helps you to avoid rebuffs and enjoy being with people.

• *Misfit Between Personality and Surroundings.* At a public lecture at one of the local universities I happened to talk to a middle-aged woman who told me that she was looking for a college graduate to marry. Her manner and conversation indicated that her intellectual level was very limited and that she was not likely to attract the sort of person she was seeking. Her misplaced goal had kept her and will continue to keep her from finding an appropriately responsive man. I have frequently seen older men come to parties wearing formal, elegant clothes when casual dress was the order of the day. The standards of their generation, together with the reluctance of many young women to socialize with older men, were frustrating and made them conspicuous.

You have to develop an intuition concerning the social niche in which you fit. Courage and daring are admirable, but there is no point in fighting odds that are totally against you. Look for emotional fulfillment among people who share your interests and goals. As those interests lead you into new areas, your circle of friends will broaden too. Of course, you can also arbitrarily decide to restructure yourself to meet some other set of social standards and plunge into a brand-new life-style. But if you aren't motivated by your own basic feelings, you may find it hard to maintain that façade.

If you are going to get some benefit from being single, if you wish to overcome emotional leprosy, then you have to know what you are doing. You have to understand your real nature, your motives, and what is essential to you before you can direct your activities toward goals that are fulfilling. You must learn to recognize people and situations that will eventually prove to be degrading. You will have to practice self-discipline, learn to avoid trivia, and perhaps change your way of life to a substantial extent. To what end?

One reward is a change in the balance between emotional emptiness and enjoyment of life. Your personality and activities will make you more attractive to a more substantial group of male and female friends.

Chapter 4

Understanding Yourself

I have talked with many singles about those areas in which they wish to develop insight. The chief questions they ask concern their feelings, how they come across to others, the reasons behind self-destructive behavior, and questions about clarifying their philosophy and values.

Social Image

If you want to establish a better social life, understanding your social image is an important first step. To a large extent your social image is a kind of visual résumé of yourself.

What creates your social image? The way you dress is an important part of it—specifically, the style, care, and coordination of various articles of clothing. There are many different ways of creating an image through clothing. When a woman does not wear a brassiere, one current interpretation of that fact might be that she is rejecting women's traditional, restricted role. Some years ago, the same behavior would have been seen as sexually provocative. The clothing people choose often reflects their self-esteem. Very elegantly dressed men and women may be telling us that they are important, attractive, and deserve to be finely adorned. Others, similarly impressive, might be covering up self-doubts, trying to substitute style for substance. The person whose clothes are poorly coordinated and inappropriate to the surroundings might be announcing poverty or lack of skill training. A bizarre combination suggests a person who is out of touch with reality or perhaps eager to shock.

Body Language

The way you carry your body is extremely revealing. Try this exercise: Right now, FREEZE IN PLACE. What message is your body conveying? Is your body leaning forward as though the message of this book is vital at the moment? Are you leaning back in a casual devil-may-care attitude? Begin to feel the various muscles of your body. Become aware of your scalp, face, neck, throat, jaw, shoulders, hands, belly, buttocks, arms, legs, hands, and feet. All of these convey a message concerning your emotional history and your current mood. When you walk into a room you often reveal by your posture whether you are overly controlled, relaxed, timid, indifferent, assertive, hostile, or whatever.

Movements also reveal what is going on inside your mind. Become aware of your jaws. You give away your anger through constant grinding movements of your teeth. If you feel yourself doing this, you are probably holding back anger, and others will see you as controlled, unspontaneous, and perhaps even hypocritical. Now, become aware of your hand movements. Are your hands always in motion? Small persistent gestures suggest that you are nervous. Larger gestures when you talk give the impression of overeagerness. As you walk, your arms stake out the amount of territory you want. Arms moving in a relaxed swing close to the body suggest a person considerate of others' rights. Others want to reserve space around them and move their arms in wide swinging motions as they walk—either aggressively or defensively.

Voice

Get into the habit of listening to yourself. If possible, tape-record a conversation with someone with whom you can be spontaneous. Many of the patients in my practice refuse to let me record their voices. It comes as a painful surprise to them to hear the intonation, pitch, intensity, pacing, and other factors that characterize their voices. Try to find out if you speak in complete sentences. One sure way to give the impression that you are uncomfortable or not very bright is to keep interjecting a meaningless phrase such as "You know." This suggests that you are too lazy to organize your thoughts or too ashamed to come right out with what is on your mind. Listen to the phrasing of your sentences. Do you lower your voice at the end so that the words are lost? Do you enunciate words carelessly and sound anxious or indifferent? Poor speech habits lessen the impact of what you are saying and can hinder both your social life and your career.

Emotional Life

It is absolutely essential to understand that emotions give us both *true* and *false* information. When a parent is responsive and encourages a child to express feelings, a unity develops between the understanding of a situation and the person's emotional life.

What interferes with this unity? What are the consequences when intellect and feelings don't coordinate? When we as children are forced to restrain our emotions or to be devious with parents and teachers, as adults we either hold back our feelings or behave deviously, or the feelings do not guide us into appropriate actions. Try to become aware of your inner self the next time you are in a group, on a date, or with a friend. Does your body feel constricted—shoulders tight, jaw clenched, breathing shallow? Are your palms clammy? These reactions point to emotional discomfort. The source, however, may not be in the present situation.

Many people guide themselves in social relationships through the ideologies and experiences of their childhood, which are often false guides to present action. When you are on a date do you find yourself responding as your parents indicated you *should* instead of reacting spontaneously to the situation at hand? You may feel put down by your companion, but tell yourself that it isn't polite to express displeasure. You have been trained not to show anger.

It is useful to monitor your feelings from time to time because they will provide *some* information as to how you are being treated. Perhaps you have no feelings at all, which would probably be an indication that the relationship is meaningless.

Many people do not tell themselves exactly why a particular person makes them uncomfortable. They may not even let themselves know that person has an effect on them, and simply experience the discomfort as a headache, nausea, or depression. They allow destructive relationships to continue because they ignore their emotional and physical reactions. As one man put it, "Why do I doubt my gut-level feelings when nine times out of ten they are correct?"

Too many singles do not take the time to study themselves to determine what their real values are. They do not have a clear philosophy of life. The consequence of this is that they drift, having momentary ups and downs, without consistent productivity, joy, constructive relationships, and everything else that follows from knowing what you really want.

The Cult of Gut Feelings

On the other hand, I have a deep skepticism about the current Cult of the Emotional. It is possible to go too far in listening to your feelings. There are those who believe that their guts are marvelous indicators of how to conduct their lives. This is baloney. In the first place, each person reacts differently. To understand your own and others' responses you must learn to be sensitive to all kinds of cues to gather information. Gut reactions are often diffuse, vague, stirred by primitive parts of the brain, affected by hormones, fatigue, and other physiological states. Your guts are conditioned to react to symbolic events. For example, rejection, overbearing authority, criticism, difficult tasks, and so on are not actually life threatening. However, to children, who are very vulnerable, they often seem so, and children quickly learn to associate unpleasant events with "gut" reactions. Because the internal organs of children are highly reactive, it is understandable that their gut reactions are conditioned to emotional events. In later life, when we experience situations that are vaguely similar to the experiences of childhood, we do not discriminate between what happened then and what is going on right now, and our conditioned reaction may be very inappropriate.

You are at a discotheque, ask a woman to dance, and she declines. Zap in the belly. She is an unknown person, of absolutely no real significance to you, yet you react intensely because her rejection symbolizes your cumulative experiences of failure. But the actual person in front of you means nothing to you.

You are on a date, and the man or woman you are with makes a comment about your clothing not being stylish or being in disarray and moves to correct it. A flush of anger comes over you and the fight is on. Stop! He or she is positively not your mother telling you you are a slob and if you don't pay more attention to your clothing you will be unlovable and never get married.

You are at a museum, and somebody is obviously hanging around with the intention of striking up a conversation. Your trained powers of observation immediately confirm that there is no resemblance between the stranger and your ideal mate. You have no immediate gut reaction, so you move along to discourage any exchange. Above all, you avoid getting any sense of the other person's style, intelligence, education, amiableness, and overall personality. But what makes you think your guts are a good guide to a satisfying relationship?

You are a woman whose father made you feel like a princess. Then finally prince charming arrived. He wined and dined you; he sent you flowers. But one terrible day, he says: "Look, my car has broken down, my bank account is a mess, could you please—just once—meet me downtown at Luigi's Pizzeria?" Your immediate thought is that the subway is terrible, buses are for peasants, you don't like to drive at night, pizza is fattening, and your guts are doing the danse macabre. No, Mr. Prince is not your father. You are not Sleeping Beauty. Grab your handbag and go!

Here is a good example of somebody who didn't attend to her feelings (or lack of them). A woman who was emotionally involved with one man also knew another man as a friend for several months. Finally she began to go out with him, and for his convenience he stayed at her home one night after a date so he wouldn't have to travel home in the wee morning hours. They did not plan to have sex, but she said that she thought it would be nice to be near a warm body at night. What did she actually feel? *"It was like sleeping with a corpse."* The woman had planned to continue this relationship until we discussed it in a therapy session. It was obvious to me that she had no real feelings for him, but she did not take this seriously. Since she had had the common experience that intense attraction at first meeting signaled disaster, she told herself that she should give the relationship a chance to develop. So far, so good. However, when she experienced (if you can call it that) no feelings for the man despite spending a night in the same bed with him, she didn't draw any conclusions from it. Actually, if you consider her statement closely, that "it was like sleeping with a corpse," you can guess that she had genuine feelings of antipathy for the man but couldn't recognize or face them. Further exploration revealed that while he was very nice to her, he was also weak, and she could make him do anything she wanted, including things that seemed unreasonable. Weakness had been a complaint of hers concerning other important men in her life. We sighed and mourned the loss of the old domineering male!

Values

Some singles have also requested clarification in the area of philosophy and values. This is a highly personal matter and more learned scholars than I have despaired of coming to any universally accepted explanations. The purpose of having a philosophy and values is to enable you to clarify the course of your own life and to avoid making certain emotionally costly errors. *Philosophy* has been defined as "The love or pursuit of wisdom . . . a system of principles for guidance in practical affairs; wise composure in dealing with problems." A closely allied system of making decisions stems from our *values*. In a sense, values determine what we find rewarding in life, but feelings toward a particular value can be both positive and negative. I have found the following list of values useful in clarifying the attitudes of those I counsel.

- Security
- Adventure
- Stability
- Variety
- Pleasure/Play
- Goal-Directedness
- Grandeur
- Simplicity
- Idealism
- Realism
- Religion
- Naturalism
- Wealth
- Career Achievement
- Altruism
- Authority

- Family
- Personal Power
- Personal Relationships
- Prestige/Recognition
- Creativity
- Culture/Esthetics
- Learning

Your values play a subtle and complex role in establishing firm relationships. They determine your positive and negative feelings toward people, situations, and ideas. Your goals are influenced by your values, because you generally work toward results that you find rewarding and compatible with your standards, and avoid situations that are distressing because they conflict with those standards. Therefore, understanding your personal values and determining their compatibility with your partner's are important steps in establishing a relationship. Reasonable agreement concerning values is necessary to sustain most relationships because values are the rewards that we seek in life.

I think that you will find it useful to think seriously about this list and decide which of these values excite and motivate you and which turn you off. For example, if you are materialistic and your potential mate feels burdened by possessions, your values are in conflict. The alternatives are compromise, struggle, or separation.

Time and the Single

Your orientation toward time is one of the most important factors in determining the way you act. It is possible to be oriented toward the past, the present, and the future at different times or simultaneously.

Some people ruminate about past events and thus exclude new people from their present. They may tell themselves that a past relationship or life situation was happy and can never be repeated or brought back. Others feel that the past was terrible, and thus they must be very cautious about the present and not make any plans for the future. Others are working through unhappy relationships, thinking about them obsessively, determined not to relate to anyone until their misery has subsided.

Other people focus narrowly on the present. They do not wish to consider any events from the past, nor do they feel the necessity of planning for the future. This can be a pleasant hedonism but ignores the changes occurring in their physical and emotional selves as well as their world. Some singles act on impulse regardless of the consequences. "I will make love right now, even though I should be finishing the project that is due tomorrow"; "I am lonely right now, so I will call _____ even though I know I'll hate myself for doing it the next day"; "I'll get drunk right now so I won't have to think about the bawling out my supervisor will give me tomorrow." One single woman I know devotes most of her time to having sex with every man she can lay her hands on because her ex-husband is slow with his alimony checks.

Equally narrow is the approach that regards only the future and ignores the fun of the present. Some people are so goal-oriented that current social contacts and simple pleasures are disregarded. One example that comes to mind is a woman who is currently devoting all of her time to employment, therapy, and studying. She feels that for the present she cannot have any fun because survival depends upon her getting a college degree as soon as possible.

Any of these extremes limits your potential for growth. The more clearly you can see your life in a total perspective, the better able you are to enjoy the present and shape the future you want. Let yourself know where you have come from, make your present a comfortable balance of fun and serious endeavor, and prepare for an emotionally fulfilling future.

Whatever your doubts and regrets, learn from the past and work toward a better future.

Chapter 5

What Do Singles Want to Know?

The most frequent question that singles ask me is: "What is a meaningful relationship?" A meaningful relationship has different qualities for different people, and recognizing this concept is the key to avoiding much misery. You have to realistically evaluate what is important for you, find out what stirs you, and then determine whether the results are emotionally satisfying.

Meaningful Relationships

Right now I want to focus on suitable relationships. Later on I will deal with the recognition of unsuitable relationships. Many unhappy people engage in relationships that are meaningful precisely because they are remarkably self-destructive. The lesson to be learned is that deep feelings and involvement by themselves are not sufficient reasons to continue seeing somebody.

I would define a meaningful relationship as one that is valuable and worth continuing because it includes mutual pleasure, shared goals, and a sense of involvement.

Yet to illustrate the diversity of opinions, here are several definitions given by people at a workshop:

• Having an interesting person to discuss things with;

• Learning about each other's intelligence, emotions, and exploring the results of new experiences;

• Going into a relationship *without* the feeling that the other person would bring me out.

A meaningful relationship for most people is more than just clinging together. As one of my clients put it, "It isn't enough to meet people who need to meet people."

WHAT CAN YOU EXPECT FROM ANOTHER PERSON? A more useful way of approaching this question is, What do you personally expect from a relationship? This can be further clarified by asking, "What do you expect of *others* and what do you expect of *yourself?*"

It is useful at an early stage to inquire about your prospective partner's desires. Some want punctuality, others stress honesty, closeness, gentleness, relaxation, kindness, energy, reciprocity, friendliness, and a wide range of other human qualities. However, you and your partner don't want generalized goodness. You each want (demand) particular qualities.

It is useful to consider briefly the problem of commitment, which relates to shared goals. To me, this is the first question to be asked (at least covertly) if you want a long-standing relationship. There are many charming guys and gals out there who are truly great on a first date and/or one-night stand but do not want continued intimacy. Thus, the key question becomes, *What degree of commitment do you and your partner wish?*

HOW HONEST SHOULD YOU BE? Even I, a psychotherapist, was shocked to hear people say at some of my open (nontherapeutic) groups that they felt they would be happiest by maintaining dishonest social relationships. I report this not because I endorse it but because this book is an honest appraisal of current attitudes. Personally, I have found that it is disastrous to start a relationship on a dishonest basis. I urge honesty as the only suitable course of action. However, you must be alert to the fact that there are plenty of dishonest, exploitative people around. Therefore, reality dictates some reasonable amount of cautiousness in new relationships.

Why are people dishonest? Sometimes they cover up their motives—sexual, economic, or whatever—which may be exploitative or damaging to the other party.

People are frequently dishonest about their level of professional success because they perceive a lack of achievement as a social liability. One person said, "If I tell the truth I'm vulnerable. I have a white lie for every occasion." As a result, this person never knows whether he is being accepted for himself or for the image he projects, which is his problem, but you nevertheless should be aware that such habitual liars exist. And they do pay a price for creating illusions. Many of those who make it their *modus operandi* acknowledge that it costs effort to create an impression and live up to expectations of strength, generosity, power, and so on. This leads to an important question.

DOES IT PAY TO BE A GIVER? Some people think they can establish a great relationship by always being obliging—trapping the other party into undying affection out of gratitude. Believe me, it doesn't work that way. I asked some people what they thought of such a constantly "giving" person. Some felt that "he/she would be likable." "I need friends, and I'm willing to help, and I'm happy if it's returned." Others felt that they would enjoy it for a while, and then see through it and be irritated or mistrustful. Quite a few expressed irritation, pity, and annoyance. "It's not human, he's a phony. . . . I can't get along with somebody like that. . . . People who have a lot going are more likely to accept people who are not always obliging. . . . At first flattered, then I would see them as a fungus on a tree, *existing for the other person.*" The implications are clear. Compulsive giving is reckless and ineffective. You will be better respected if you express your own needs and are reasonably self-protective. Assigning to yourself the role of being strong, of being the chronic giver, ignores your own emotional need to receive support as well as to give it. It is quite possible to create within yourself the false impression of strength, and then pick friends who confirm that image. There may be an unexpected crisis in your life when you will come to grips with the fact that you are emotionally unsatisfied. You may then find that there is no one around to fulfill your needs.

What about sexual relationships? If you are the giver, you will be expected to cater consistently to your partner. In this way you train the other party to be passive and weak. Bitter experiences can result, because even when you are needy, your partner will expect you to continue to function as before. If you decide that you want reciprocity or want to be the taker for a while, your partner is likely to consider that a *betrayal*.

Your attitude toward giving and taking is generally determined by experiences in your early life. One woman said about herself: "My parents leaned on me. I gave them all I could. I still feel that I have to be the mother. I feel that I'm doing all the giving and getting nothing in return. My former friends made me important by needing me. Now I have a compulsive urge to help. This keeps me from expressing my anger and running away."

Another woman expected the man to be the giver: "He was half angel and half devil. I wanted to be associated with a superior man. I was in love with him. I was in it for exploitation. With him there were places and people I had access to that I wouldn't have otherwise."

WHAT ABOUT EMOTIONAL DEPENDENCY? It is easy to conceal frustrated dependency needs from yourself. They originate at the very beginning of life, and you learn to cope with them early. Emotional hunger becomes so familiar that it often goes unrecognized. Nevertheless, it has a profound effect, leading you to unconsciously manipulate others to assuage that hunger. If you are unaware of your needs, then you are also unaware that you want people to fill those needs. You may go through all kinds of unwitting emotional contortions to get satisfaction and not recognize that your neediness may repel others.

On the other hand, feeling intensely emotionally deprived and lonely can lead to equally self-defeating patterns—among them pursuing relationships with inappropriate people. Some people find loneliness so oppressive that they will do anything rather than be alone, including putting up with all kinds of shabby treatment. Others react in ways that make their loneliness even worse. One women reported that, "When I'm disappointed by someone who's important to me, I go into a depression and withdraw from everyone." Another person is even more self-destructive. He says, "When I'm blue, depressed, lonely, I don't want anybody to like me."

One of the keys to handling or, better yet, preventing such loneliness and depression is to surround yourself with supportive people. Begin today to identify those people who don't add to your life—and get them out of your life. Start learning to recognize and make contact with people who will have a positive effect, who will bring out the best in you, which includes your own capacity to take an interest in other people's welfare.

Emotional common sense tells you that you should not put up with self-destructive relationships in the name of friendship or family!

HOW SPECIFIC SHOULD YOU BE IN ASKING QUESTIONS? The answer to this question is tied up with your social sensitivity and your hidden agenda. Questions serve a number of different purposes. They carry on a conversation. They reveal your interest in people and their activities. They enable you to obtain information about a new acquaintance's status, needs, intentions, feelings about you, and so on. There are people who can uncover all sorts of intimate details about virtual strangers through a constant barrage of questions, which seemingly are not resented. And they know after a relatively brief time whether there is a possibility for a relationship or not.

Yet, asking too many, or the wrong, questions can arouse resentment. You must be aware of the other person's mood and monitor their expressions as you proceed. If you see signs that your questions are unwelcome, stop. Pay attention to facial features, tone of voice, the completeness of the answer, any tendency to be evasive or to change the subject.

Have a good reason for asking questions. If your chief reason is having sex that night, or avoiding it, then some issues might have to be confronted immediately. However, if you are comfortable with the person and intuitively see that there are possibilities for a relationship, the hazards of putting off the interrogation are minimal. A later date might be a suitable occasion. Nevertheless, it is a good idea to establish as soon as possible whether there is the basis for a relationship or if insurmountable barriers exist.

"WHAT DO YOU DO?" By analyzing people's feelings about this question we can look closely at the dynamics of beginning a relationship.

Since many people are conditioned to stereotype people by their occupation, if you ask about someone's occupation, what reaction can you expect? You may be perceived as a snob, setting standards for the other person to match. Some people fear that they will be categorized in your mind according to their answer. Others worry about being sized up financially and will answer your question to avoid seeming rude, but they may resent it. Many feel that they have other valuable qualities, apart from their occupation. Some are ashamed of their occupation. Still others want to keep their social life entirely separate from their business life and won't talk about their work at all.

There are sometimes valid reasons for inquiring into a new acquaintance's occupation, although timing is important. Most people have fairly specific ideas as to the kind of person they can relate to. They feel comfortable with a partner whose standards of education, affluence, interests, intelligence, and so on are compatible with theirs.

It is probably good form not to use the question "What do you do?" as an icebreaker unless you find yourself terribly short of time and are taking risks to screen out time-wasting individuals. Whether or not to answer such a question can be accepted in the same spirit. In the process of exploring a relationship, it is too important a matter to be concealed, although poor pacing can blow the whole business and evasion means running the risk of looking as though you have something to hide. Should you answer, observe carefully the other person's reactions.

"Have you ever been married?" Some people believe that your eligibility can be judged from your track record. They evaluate a new acquaintance as if they were analyzing a card for the Kentucky Derby. You cannot avoid prejudices and preferences, so it is better to express the facts and see how your inquisitor reacts.

HOW CRITICAL SHOULD YOU BE? It is extremely important to foster an atmosphere of openness in any significant relationship. When you care about somebody, you don't want to second-guess what is on his or her mind. The best way to begin to establish an intimate relationship is to express your feelings and to exchange ideas freely. In the course of doing that, however, conflict may arise because there is a definite, perhaps irremediable, incompatibility. Hostility may not be expressed openly but the message that comes across is: "I don't like you any more." At that point it becomes impossible to get useful information. The reasons for rejection can be dishonest and destructive to your self-esteem. It may be reasonable and self-protective to recognize the antagonism, sever the relationship, and begin anew with somebody else rather than try to resolve the conflict.

SHOULDN'T YOU LOOK FOR THE GOOD IN PEOPLE? No! If you have to make an effort to look, either it isn't there or there are so many neurotic hang-ups that any generous, loving qualities are hidden. I know one woman who entered into a series of poor relationships because she sought out the person's good qualities and ignored what made these men poison for her. You should only maintain relationships with people who have a beneficial effect on your feelings and well-being. What is poison for the next guy might be marvelous for you and vice versa.

WHAT DO PEOPLE CARRY OVER INTO A NEW RELATIONSHIP? The answer is *plenty!* You are shaped by your parents' training and values, by your frustated expectations early in life, by your expectation that certain kinds of satisfaction will continue, and by the fact that your unconscious works overtime to elaborate, distort, and connect many of your experiences (related or not!).

Transference from one situation to another occurs because you develop tunnel vision. You have a few stirring experiences and then expect all others to turn out the same way. A few rejections and you are gun-shy at the next party. Or you have a bad experience in an intimate relationship, and when someone new comes along with a single characteristic that reminds you of the person who hurt you, you redirect your hostility and reject the possibility of giving the new person a chance. Your social track record will improve when you learn what your stereotypes are and fight them. Learn not to generalize, not to judge all new experiences on the basis of a few bad experiences in the past.

One classic example of someone who carries the past into all present situations is an attractive man with a quick mind, a sense of humor, and keen intelligence. He feels that he is given a quick shuffle by women, who don't take him seriously. He has developed a bitter, cynical wit and feels mistreated by women because he is convinced that they merely tolerate him and have no genuine interest in him.

In describing his childhood, he recalls that his parents would say "You're a nice boy," but he believes that underneath their real beliefs were "You're not too sharp. Don't be conspicuous—just have modest ambitions. You're really a shlep. It's not so bad."

What is his reaction to all this? "I have bad feelings about myself, and while I know it's objectively untrue that I'm a worthless person, the feelings stay with me. Sometimes the temptation to be antisocial is strong. With women I feel ignored and not taken seriously. I feel better when I speak my mind." When he does so, he often overreacts, escalating a problem situation beyond reconciliation.

WHEN SOMETHING GOES WRONG, HOW MUCH BLAME IS YOURS AND HOW MUCH IS THE OTHER PERSON'S? There are so many ways in which a relationship can go sour! Deliberate mistreatment or exploitation is quite common. People seek outlets for their hostility, take undue advantage, are aware that they are inconsiderate, pick away at weak spots, and so on.

Much hostility is partially hidden both from the aggressor and from the victim. A woman who read one of my books disagreed that teasing is largely hostile. Then she thought of an uncle of hers who was very athletic. He enjoyed flicking out his leg rapidly so that somebody would trip over him unexpectedly. "You know, now that I think about it, falling really hurt! Maybe teasing is hostile," she commented.

You may not be aware of the resentment that you create or experience. When the explosion takes place, the cause is obscure because it seems exaggerated in terms of the immediate situation. On the other hand, you or the other person could probably point out a long history of seemingly small digs and insensitivities.

Some relationships are stressful because the parties have a serious incompatibility. They are different kinds of people, and in trying to fulfill each other's needs, basic desires or personality traits have to be compromised or completely suppressed. If you love fine art or music or sports or hunting and are in a relationship with somebody who dislikes these activities, you either have to participate alone or try to educate the person to enjoy it. If this cannot be done, then there is a struggle for power or resentment at being deprived. Who is to blame? Nobody. The hazard of such a relationship should be carefully evaluated before you become committed. It is important to recognize self-destructive relationships, which are discussed in the next chapter.

Chapter 6

Recognizing
Self-destructive Relationships

The most remarkable observation I have made in more than twenty years of psychological practice, leading human relations workshops and just observing nature, is the amount of torture and punishment that people inflict and put up with in the name of love.

Love Can Be Self-destructive

It is amazing that so many men and women persist in love affairs, marriages, friendships, job situations, and other relationships that are frustrating, humiliating, hopeless, and generally unrewarding. People are more self-destructive in their "love" relationships than in any others. The resulting emotional disturbances are extremely stressful. Since most people expect more pleasure from love than from any other experience, why do they engage in relationships that create havoc in their emotional life, prevent growth, and interfere with their ability to carry on in careers, hobbies, education, and other important activities? What makes them vulnerable to participating in this chronic form of misery? This chapter offers guidelines to recognizing self-destructive relationships that cannot be mended, and how to avoid them.

Sadomasochistic Relationships

A self-destructive relationship is one that ignores or violates your basic requirements, lacks warmth, is impervious to change, and leaves you unfulfilled or actively unhappy. But it sometimes seems that for every sadist, there is a willing masochist. The way you learned to settle fights and to express anger when you were growing up are significant factors in determining how you react to destructive situations today. Learning to handle anger is one of the most important elements in shaping your personality.

People could not get away with being brutal in their social and business contacts unless others were trained to accept degradation and rotten behavior. If you are vulnerable, it is because you never learned how to protect yourself and that you have a right to decent treatment. Consequently, you stay in downgrading situations.

Why do sadomasochistic relationships develop and continue? Sadists displace their anger, aiming it at people who have never harmed them and away from those who brutalized them as children. Masochists are afraid to demonstrate their anger directly. They need mistreatment to justify their reproach against those who were cruel and disappointed them in childhood.

Let me offer some examples of self-destructive relationships.

• A woman had a relationship with a man for eight years while he was living with his wife and children. They generally saw each other during weekends if he did not have any family obligations. He told her that he loved her, but that he didn't want to hurt his wife and children by leaving. When he finally left his wife he refused to spend any more time with the woman than he had before, saying that he needed a period of freedom. He made arrangements to share a beach house with a group of people, assuming that she wouldn't mind if he spent most of the weekends with his son and the friend who was sharing his room. She could find sleeping quarters elsewhere in the house during a few weekends of the summer. He was very puzzled when she was hurt by this arrangement. One day she discovered that she was pregnant. It was inconvenient for him to be with her either the night before or the day she had the abortion. She was resentful and felt abandoned, but her tolerance for this sort of punishment diminished very slowly. Two years after the termination of the relationship she was still reluctant to date other men.

• A married man with two children remained with his wife for several decades despite her coldness. She criticized him, spent as much time as possible with her parents who lived nearby, and refused to have sex with him. Feeling utterly devalued in his personal life was damaging to his professional life, and he let himself be caught in a vicious cycle. Only when his children were in college, and after years of therapy, was he able to tell his wife that their marriage was through.

• A woman had a relationship with a man for almost ten years. During the last years they lived in the same apartment but had no sexual contact. This living arrangement gave her no privacy or opportunity to develop other relationships. During the latter years, the man slid backwards professionally. He abandoned his career and tried to earn a living by chess hustling. When the woman finally decided to move, she implied that he could join her later, but really didn't want him to. When he saw her apartment he wanted the best room for himself. While she did not permit him to move in with her, she tortures herself with the belief that she did him a great injustice, and thinks that eventually he will straighten himself out.

• A young man maintains a relationship with a woman who makes him feel "hemmed in, strangled, depressed." He reports that, "As an executive, she has to project a firm image. She isn't bossy, but her tone of voice turns me off. She sounds like a sales director, not a girl friend. She tells me I'm not assertive enough, but I don't want her to tell me in such an assertive tone." When asked why he couldn't tell her his feelings, he replied, "I get chest pains." Not surprisingly, his mother has always lectured him and told him what to do.

You can learn to recognize more clearly some of the signs of emotional discomfort that signal a destructive relationship, but there is a trap to avoid. It is easy to identify the rotten things being done to you and to ignore the destruction you dish out to somebody else. Recognizing destructive emotional effects can alert you to the hostility in your own nature. It is equally self-destructive to deliberately or unconsciously act in a damaging way toward other people.

Loss of Peace of Mind

Perhaps the earliest sign of a self-destructive relationship is the feeling that your well-being is disturbed. You may find yourself being deliberately provocative, reacting in one of the following ways—a husband to his wife: "What are you burning for dinner?" One man acknowledges, "I stir people up for excitement." Another says "I prod the other person to dislike me and be nasty so that I can break it off." One person was provocative because "I need to be independent and not accepted." It makes someone else "feel good when people are angry with me." One woman used insults to prevent her marriage from improving so that she wouldn't be disappointed if anything went wrong.

This sort of thing is why one person recommended "combat training for the courtship ritual." Looking at it another way, "some relationships are like strychnine pie," a few grains are poison.

Be alert to chronic anger, depression, tension, headaches, anxiety, and so on. Some people develop sexual problems such as impotence or frigidity.

Disturbed Self-esteem

Most people consciously strive toward self-respect and self-acceptance, but they may unconsciously sabotage those goals. Be alert for feelings of being rejected and/or downgraded directly or indirectly. Avoid people who constantly make you feel that you are a failure; that kind of message, whether open or hidden, can diminish your self-image and impair your effectiveness.

If you find that you are always insecure in a particular relationship, you inevitably will wonder about your partner's fidelity and dependability. It is self-destructive to remain in a situation in which you are always getting signals that you are not desired!

Unreasonable Demands

Feeling persistently asked to do or give more than you can indicates a serious mismatch between you and the other person. There may be a struggle for power. Emotional emptiness or dependency can also create demands. Paradoxically, an extremely dependent person can have trouble forming a close relationship because no amount of reassurance fills that person's need for love and support.

Another sign of being involved with an unreasonably demanding person is the feeling that you are always placating in order to maintain peace. Jealousy is yet another way of making unacceptable demands for loyalty.

Sometimes you create situations of stress through your own manipulations. One man said: "I get hurt and anxious because my girl friend is so jealous. She feels bad if I go out with someone else. I'm afraid to tell her in a straightforward way that I want to do this. Sometimes in an ecstatic moment I say, 'My penis belongs to you.' " He acknowledged that he created "situations in which I am torn between two extremes. I want it to be good for me and also good for her." His self-destructiveness comes from not being honest with his girl friend and exaggerating his loyalty.

Being involved with a demanding person can leave you feeling depleted. One man commented that, "My wife couldn't tolerate my being alone with music. She has an insatiable need to be reassured and felt abandoned. I felt totally swamped and oppressed. Even two years of marriage counseling and group therapy didn't help. I always gave in and I was not doing what was vital to me. I became resentful and angry with myself. I had to get out of that relationship." Another man, recently separated, had a similar complaint: "My wife has a tremendous need to be with people and have attention. I commuted and came home late. My career is important to me. She always wanted me to me with her. 'Don't work late, stay with me,' she'd plead." His parents had always fought; he had hated the turmoil and as a result he would go to great lengths to avoid conflict.

Giving in to unreasonable demands also makes you feel exploited. As one woman recounted, "The first three times Jim took me out we had dinner in a nice restaurant and danced. Now all we do is come to my house and make love. He never takes me out. He claims he has no money because of what he pays for child support. He doesn't even take me for a walk." Why does she bother with him? Because she is so vulnerable to loneliness.

When the demands are excessive, you can feel powerless, but there is no need to reach that point if you stay alert to the warning signals.

Needs Unfulfilled

The basic needs of most people include the need for love, sexual fulfillment, recognition, and companionship. Therefore, it is very self-destructive to participate in a relationship in which most of your needs remain unfulfilled. Of course, you have to first assess whether your needs are really excessive, resulting from emotional deprivation while you were growing up. You cannot expect a friend or lover to compensate for early frustration, nor to do for you emotionally what adults do for themselves. Psychotherapy could be a healing experience and help you avoid destroying relationships by clutching unacceptably.

The need for closeness is basic, but people differ considerably in this regard. To become involved with somebody who cannot offer you what you want is self-defeating, and to persist suggests that you are trying to undo frustrating experiences with an ungiving parent.

Here is how a man with a fear of closeness described himself: "I get terrified by her needs. I have difficulty giving in intimate situations. I'm afraid that she can control me by her anxieties. If she yells I feel impotent and get very cold. I have a fear of intimacy." Another person stated openly: "My relationships are pleasant, but they don't go POW. They don't go anyplace. I play it very safe and don't take any risks. I don't get involved." Other comments have included, "I have learned to be distrustful of women," and "I pick independent women so they won't make demands and lean on me." These variations on the theme of fear of intimacy and closeness ought to be signals for the person who wants closeness. One woman maintained that "only fighting makes the relationship work." This was an indirect way of saying that she and her partner were not close, and she could only involve him through aggression. Some people reared in abusive households are conditioned to exaggerate aggression to convey commonplace feelings.

It is not quite correct to say that everybody has the same needs. Although the *kind* of needs are the same, the intensity of specific needs differs from person to person. This is determined by your particular constitution, your experiences while growing up, how much acceptance you had, whether you were encouraged to mature, and so on. One person may have a considerable emotional deficit and need a great deal of love. That person's fulfillment may be blocked by the other's inability to be expressive or by a preoccupation with something outside the relationship. Sometimes one person's deprivation is so strong that reasonable attentiveness is insufficient to satisfy. I have known several people whose infantile needs for closeness created tremendous conflict in their love relationships. Significantly, in each of these cases, the other person knew early in the relationship of the depth of that person's frustrations and demands, and chose to ignore it.

Inhibited Emotional Expression and Development

Sometimes your normal desire to express anger or emotional pain is discouraged or forbidden because it would reveal the injustice of another person's behavior. One woman described her pattern as follows: "He refused to allow me to tell him when I was angry or affectionate. He couldn't tell me he didn't want me with him. If I express anger, I am afraid that the other person will leave me as my father did." She was also hampered in coming to grips with this man because of transferred fear.

A relationship that hampers the expression of feelings is static. It does not change or grow. When one person actively resists closeness or the exchange of affection, the other partner is not permitted to show his or her feelings and develop a stronger bond. It is self-destructive not to tell the other person when you feel prohibited from expressing yourself. The feeling of frustration is likely to cause permanent estrangement through resentment.

Handling emotional pain and anger. How to handle pain and anger is learned at home while growing up. Most people are trained not to express those feelings for fear of hurting their parents. Some individuals, however, grow up in households that encourage open expression of feelings. They have learned to be assertive through the models their parents presented, and the acceptance they themselves received. Two people who have been reared in such households feel perfectly at home with each other. However, those who have grown up in emotion-inhibiting households have been trained not to express strong emotions of any kind and don't know how to handle unrestrained feelings. They may be overwhelmed by a normally assertive person and virtually terrorized by an emotionally uninhibited person whose behavior verges on the abusive. An abusive person often does not realize he or she is behaving in an emotionally dangerous way. If you find yourself in such a relationship it is important for you to distinguish between acceptable and unacceptable forms of expression. Let the other person know where you stand. If you remain in a damaging situation, you have only yourself to blame, though, admittedly, taking action is not easy.

Many people have great difficulty expressing emotional pain, hurt, or humiliation. But the result of holding back these feelings over a period of time is depression, withdrawal, and sudden outbursts of hidden anger that will eventually destroy any relationship.

The relationship between lack of identity and passivity. If you don't know who you are, then you don't know what you want and how to get what you want. If you have not developed self-understanding, you are condemned to do what other people want. Start getting to know yourself or you will remain dissatisfied because you always yield to somebody else. Once you know what to ask for you will begin to get satisfaction.

Powerlessness. Some of you believe that your wishes are unimportant; consequently, you don't think that you can have any influence on the people around you. This is clearly self-destructive, so try to recognize the attitude and avoid people who take advantage of your weakness and discourage you from developing your identity and feelings of value. If you let yourself feel pushed around, the responsibility for sabotaging the relationship is as much yours as the other person's. Don't put your ego in other people's hands. Recognize your self-worth and the fact that you have alternatives.

Discrepant Life-styles and Values

When there are basic disagreements between the way you and another person experience the world, it is difficult to form a satisfactory relationship. Then, even two people of goodwill cannot make a go of it.

Your life-style is the overall way in which you organize your life. It is as unique as your signature. Often it is determined by the models presented you as a child or by your determination to avoid the frustrations and pains of your youth. With such deep commitments, it is no surprise that you find it hard to accommodate sharply divergent life-styles in others.

For example, if you crave the material security that money represents and the other person is indifferent or hostile to financial achievement, a resolution is hard to imagine. It is self-destructive to form permanent relationships with people whose needs, values, priorities, or goals are so different from yours that you are irritated, frustrated, or antagonized. One man I know complained that when he took a woman to a good restaurant she was disdainful because the restaurant didn't require reservations!

Values and goals are the attitudes that shape your life. It is doubtful that you can achieve emotional fulfillment unless the outcome of your efforts is experienced as valuable or rewarding. It follows that if two people have different values and goals, their relationship will prove to be personally frustrating. To avoid that frustration, you owe it to yourself to be clear about your own needs as well as the other person's and not delude yourself into thinking you can alter someone else's attitudes.

Temperamental Differences

One of the chief qualities that creates a bond or a wedge between people is the intangible kind of emotional expression called temperament. Even at birth infants differ in their temperament. Traits of excitability, calmness, persistence, changeability, high or low energy, courage or fearfulness, sociability or withdrawal, are deeply ingrained and are resistant to change by the time a person reaches adulthood.

If someone's temperament rubs you the wrong way, the chances for a satisfying relationship are slight. No amount of agreement on politics or friends will create a bond when the way you express your feelings creates discomfort. When one of you wants to get up and go, and the other likes to lounge in bed, somebody suffers. What seem like minor differences are not so easily resolved, so don't take on the frustrations of a relationship with a temperamentally unsuitable person.

Chapter 7

Why Self-destruction?

Why do people permit acts of degradation against themselves in their sexual relationships? (Many of the same reasons apply to family, employers, and other areas of life.)

Hiding Your Real Feelings

Let's start by examining some of the rationalizations people offer for remaining in destructive relationships. Here are some typical comments:

"I became totally involved with this man, but he, like most men, is into his work." (The hidden statement is, "He doesn't pay much attention to me. I must avoid looking at the fact that he is uninterested. It is easier to think of him as a loyal employee advancing his career than to permit my ego to be hurt by realizing he just doesn't care about me.")

"I can never get a sexual relationship as good as this. No sex-manual ideal can match our lovemaking." ("My neurosis makes me really hard to please and this person puts up with me.")

"I remember how lovely it was at the beginning of our relationship, even though I sometimes have to put up with a lot of crap now." ("I never could size up people and I've made another error in judgment, but I can't face the reality that what I want and what I have are not the same.")

"If I drop this relationship, my lover will fall apart." ("I personally will die of guilt.")

"The relationship will change. I can't believe that it's failing." ("I am, always have been, and always will be, unlovable. This affair is a further proof of it.")

"It must be satisfying some need. To speed up my analysis, and thus my personal growth, I'll stick with it until I find out what is really making me suffer." ("I'm really a masochist and no amount of suffering can cause me to seek happier experiences.")

"I'm a failure if I admit that the relationship is over." ("I have been bragging to all my friends. They will laugh themselves sick at my expense if I tell them what really has been happening.")

"I can't hurt the other person. I'll wait until he/she makes the break." ("I am and always will be a coward.")

"Maybe it's going to change." ("I'm an incurable optimist. It conceals my basic inability to learn from experience.")

There are a number of significant reasons why people form alliances that destroy their peace of mind and prevent their personal growth.

Emotional Emptiness (Lack of Autonomy)

Autonomy may be defined as the capacity to function effectively as a separate person. The autonomous person does enjoy intimate relationships with other people but is not totally dependent on them.

Most of us have been propagandized to believe that the only suitable life is based upon marriage. The result is vulnerability to depression, desolation, and the terror of being alone.

People who lack autonomy are dependent on others for approval because they haven't learned to feed themselves emotionally. Frequently, they do not value the worth of their personality and productivity. Overdependent people tend to manipulate others for approval and love because they never dream of offering it to themselves or deciding that there are other things in life besides love and approval. Such people tend to become "clutchers." They often will settle for any warm body because they expect to be judged defective if they do not have a mate. They may even partly recognize the fallacy of this and berate themselves, making their emotional life even worse. If you discover this tendency in yourself, you should explore whether it has led you to cling to people who are unsuitable.

Emotional emptiness is a crucial motivating factor in forming bad relationships. The emotionally empty person is intolerably unhappy unless he or she receives constant emotional nourishment from others. If you have not been trained to develop personal resources, or if demands have been made on you to care for the needs of others, you may have grown up feeling emotionally depleted. Consequently, you depend on anybody who offers you emotional sustenance.

It is possible, of course, that for brief periods another person can relieve your emotional emptiness. At one point in Vincent van Gogh's generally miserable life he commented on his relationship with a woman: "She and I are two unhappy people who keep together; this way unhappiness is changed to joy and the unbearable becomes bearable."

People who crave affection feel that they are nothing without love from another. One woman said: "Not to have sex is not to have anybody love me and show me affection. This means that I am unwanted and therefore not lovable." Another woman, who insisted on marrying a man who had disregarded her emotional needs for closeness, and openly chased other girls during their adolescent courtship, put it this way: "I want other people to feel about me the way I feel about them. . . . I spent most of my life caring for other people." I asked her what she liked about herself, and she said that she was "truthful, honest, and sincere." What was unlikable? "I don't take time out for myself. This would be letting other people know my importance." She exists emotionally only when she is doing something for others.

Someone else said, "I will have nothing if I leave him, nothingness is terrible." Another unhappy example: "I only feel important when I'm going with a man I like and who likes me. Otherwise I feel like I take up no space on the sidewalk. I feel like an empty well when I'm not seeing someone." Not only women feel this way. A man reported that "When I have a woman, I do better in business."

Emotional emptiness creates a craving for companionship, which makes you particularly vulnerable to accepting companionship indiscriminately, and therefore becoming involved with unsuitable people.

Emotional emptiness also can be self-created. Be aware of self-destructive tendencies to become resentful and feel unappreciated by other people. If you feel you're always on the giving end, but not getting the praise or attention you want, ask yourself whether the other person wants your generosity or if you are using it to buy his or her affection.

Some people don't feed their own egos. A voice from the past tells them to "wait" before doing something for themselves. One man from an immigrant family said, "I'm giving all the time. I don't indulge myself. Everything goes to my ex-wife and children. I don't want my children to have the same deprivation I had." So in fulfilling what he perceives to be his obligations he prolongs his own deprivation. As a result, he has little to offer either emotionally or materially to anyone new in his life.

Emotionally empty people are often self-appointed martyrs. A healthier attitude is reflected in the following comments. "I don't think that a relationship should involve sacrificing everything I have. I want to be me. I don't want to change because somebody wants me to give more than I care to. If I or my partner feel that we're sacrificing, it's resented. It's a weapon we would end up using against each other." This sums it up pretty well. You do need others to feed you once in a while, and others need the same from you, but there has to be a comfortable balance between giving and taking.

Fear of Rejection

Intense vulnerability to rejection usually is created early in life by rebuffs, which are now irrelevant but continue to plague you on an unconscious level and lower your self-esteem. It is not unusual to carry over feelings from earlier life as though they were still valid. Then when you are being mistreated as an adult you are afraid to stand up for your right to better treatment. Children don't have much choice but you as an adult do.

Feelings of oversensitivity can prevent you from having positive new experiences; they also make you cowardly in your dealings with others. A patient of mine reported, "I get hurt very easily. Even with a hint of rejection I go off the deep end. A woman I knew casually walked away from me at a party and I was off-balance for the rest of the evening." If you tend to react as this man did, you know your rejection threshold needs to be raised.

Some people displace their own fears by projecting them onto others. Under the guise of not hurting somebody else, they avoid creating any situation in which opposition might occur. Such people avoid establishing any close relationships.

To expect rejection is a total reversal of human nature. If we weren't taken care of when we came into the world we would immediately perish. Our species, and our civilization, has evolved through the cooperation of the family and the immediate community. Our world has become structured in such a way that most material goods and spiritual wealth are obtained through contact with others. The person who expects rejection is self-excluded from much of the best part of life. Overly sensitive people feel defenseless. It is as though they have no barriers between themselves and hostile actions. They do not discriminate between what happens outside themselves, and their person. Criticism is perceived as absolutely accurate and damaging. It is not an opinion but a fact, which immediately reaches their guts. Another form of oversensitivity is total empathy with the feeling of pain that other people experience. Such people are unable to express anger or rejection because they will feel it as intensely as the person at whom it is directed. Therefore, even undesirable or self-destructive relationships are maintained unmodified.

People who fear rejection are extremely hampered in expressing their feelings. As a child you may have learned first to hold back emotional pain, then anger, and ultimately not to even express warmth and love. As a result, others may perceive you as inhibited, cold, or frightened, and those who want warmth are not likely to be attracted to you. The people who enter your life are those who enjoy being bullies or who want to avoid any emotional demands. Fearful, sensitive individuals can be demanding in indirect, covert ways, which also create conflicts.

The possibility of rejection is experienced differently by various people. Some refuse to be frightened. For others, rejection is so painful that they avoid any social contacts. Vulnerability can be experienced as "a fear of being devoured" or being exploited "if I reveal my desperation." Fortunately, most people don't go to the extreme of the woman who would arrive at a party, and before going in, avoid all danger by telling herself, "That was fun, let's go home."

Is it true that announcing your vulnerability invites attack or rejection? There *are* people who take advantage of inviting targets, and we will discuss this later in the chapter on anger. Nevertheless, it is vital to be relatively honest about weaknesses as well as strengths but to stage-manage your life in such a way as to have more positive experiences and associates. It is equally important to recognize people who are genuinely critical and degrading and to eliminate them without exception from your life.

Self-degradation

Hateful thoughts about yourself are allied with fear of rejection. In one case you expect others to dislike you; in the other, you do the hatchet job yourself. Some people are like sponges, sopping up all the abuse they experienced while growing up, and then refusing to relinquish thoughts and feelings that hamper them as adults in every possible area of life. A strange paradox arises. The self-degrading person is afraid to meet others and is also afraid to be alone. Such people, when they feel trapped in their homes, cry, feel nauseous, experience vague terrors. They fight their feelings through tranquilizers, sleeping pills, drinking, and going to bed early. They call up people for momentary relief, even though the relationship is poor. New fuel is added to the old fires. The habit of seeing yourself as valueless, perhaps even hateful, may make you insensitive to terrible treatment.

Some people even court mistreatment unconsciously. When you degrade yourself, there are several consequences. You become depressed, you make demands on others for reassurance, and you present yourself as undesirable, so that the people you most want to reach are likely to avoid you.

Learn to recognize signs of self-hatred. The following comments may strike a familiar chord.

"I try to prove myself to my boyfriend. I give him things and he tells me that he doesn't reciprocate gifts. My mother used to tell me that I'm ungrateful." (Here, the derogatory picture of herself causes her to try to buy affection and to take the blame for her own feelings when her goodwill is not reciprocated. She stays with somebody who is not emotionally expressive in a way she would appreciate.)

"Even though I earn $20,000 a year, I feel like a kid and a piece of crap." (Realistic achievement does not eliminate this person's belief in her worthlessness.)

"I blame myself if anything goes wrong in a relationship." (Only somebody who feels like a total incompetent would always accept the onus of failure.)

"I feel wiped out when I'm away from the person I'm involved with." (In addition to feelings of worthlessness, and being defined by and given value by a partner, this person lacks enjoyment of his own person and ability to function alone.)

Your self-image and sense of value are influenced by how others treat you. Critical parents, destructive teachers, the cruel comments of other children, and so on create a sensitivity to criticism. As a child you may have identified with the hostility and accepted your critics' comments. These painful messages became part of your identity. If you start by believing that you are a bad child, you end up by telling yourself you are no good, weak, valueless, unlovable, and all the other forms of criticism that you have been exposed to. People with low self-esteem are particularly vulnerable to self-destructive relationships.

This was summarized by one person as follows: "When I knock down my self-esteem, it keeps me in relationships I don't want and out of relationships I do want."

Perhaps you can identify with some of these statements:

"My weight and drinking are dependent upon whether I'm happy. My self-esteem depends on external circumstances."

"I seek out sick people."

"Only when a man pays attention to me do I bloom."

"I stay with schnooks."

"I don't feel likable. How can I get someone to like me? I may try to express my feelings, but if the other person doesn't agree or objects, I back off. It's just another unlikable thing about me."

"Not liking myself well enough makes me dependent. I can't be on my own. I allow myself to need too much. I give in to people, put myself in a less independent light."

Guilt

Guilty feelings are a prominent aspect of self-degradation. I am not proposing that you take no responsibility for what you do to others. The current cult of "you do your thing and I do mine" can be utilized as an excuse to exploit people. On the other hand, some parents manipulate their children by making them feel unnecessary guilt, and the victims of such manipulative behavior often come to believe that they are bad, and therefore worthless and entitled to nothing. To feel chronic guilt means that one part of your mind is angry with another for being evil or doing terrible things. A variety of self-destructive acts and destructive acts directed at others result from this anger. Sometimes you project your own feelings of guilt onto others, accusing them of doing what you would dearly like to do.

Passivity

The inability to insist on what you want and to influence people in important ways usually results from self-hatred.

Here is how some people describe their passivity:

"I give other people control. My spirits go up and down according to what other people do to me."

"Rather than take a position, I give in to the other person."

"I am too passive. My girl friends call me sometimes when they are depressed and I let them drag me into their depression. I want somebody to drag me into happiness."

"In any relationship I end up by being obsequious."

"I let other people lie to me."

"I can't talk back when somebody says something rotten to me."

This is a competitive world, inhabited by large numbers of selfish, hostile, domineering people. When you don't assert yourself, you allow yourself to be pushed around and deprived of the things you want. Be aware of the trap some insecure people set up—casting somebody else in the inferior role in order to feel superior by comparison. This game requires people who need to humiliate others and targets who do not defend themselves.

Assertiveness depends upon having some sense of identity. When you are passive, you let your actions be determined by the wishes and needs of others. Unless you can assert yourself, it is impossible to fulfill your needs and reach your goals.

Fear of Authority

Fear of authority creates all kinds of circumstances that diminish your self-esteem and prevent you from creating a life-style you can enjoy.

Do you react as these people did?

"I am afraid to bring the man I'm dating home because my parents won't like him."

"I often work late at the office, because my boss asks me at the last minute. Consequently, I can't make any definite plans."

"I went to speak to my super, and he started complaining to me about the tenants. He said he's there to represent the management. I'm afraid to corner him and get him to make repairs even though my apartment is a wreck."

Your fears can keep you surrounded by a lot of undesirable, tyrannical people who exert inappropriate authority over you. One person understood this very well: "I let them be powerful. I made them powerful in my own mind."

There are many ways of developing healthy assertiveness, including psychotherapy, human-relations workshops, various self-help books, and, above all, by resolutely associating only with people who are encouraging and bring out the best feelings in you. People who care about you want you to develop your own individuality.

Transference From Early Life

Just about everyone has certain fantasies, attitudes, and feelings that originated in the distant past, are no longer applicable, but continue to influence present behavior.

Here are some examples of this sort of transference:

"I've learned to be distrustful of women/men." (Previous experiences, even if misinterpreted, have become overgeneralized.)

"I keep getting involved with difficult, emotionally cut-off people. My father didn't communicate his feelings, and it is a challenge to get them to be attentive to me." (This person tries to undo earlier frustrations by re-creating the past in the present.)

"I anticipate that the worst that can happen will happen."

(Early failure, rejection, and a negative atmosphere are expected to continue.)

"I have come to expect ingratitude. My father never paid me a compliment in his life. I do a lot for people and they say, 'Oh, that's nothing.' " (This person selects individuals who take her for granted.)

"My mother told me that when you live at home your parents take care of you. When you're married, your husband takes care of you." (She developed unreal expectations that others would assume responsibility for her well-being.)

Love at First Sight

A lot of people get upset when I assert that love at first sight is a symptom of self-deception. To me, love at first sight is an extension of adolescent daydreams, which developed at a time of youthful confusion and dependency. When these daydreams persist into adulthood you expect the object of your affections to follow a private script that you wrote years before. You then tend to demand, manipulate, and provoke guilt to get what you want, ignoring the fact that the other person does not know your private agenda. This self-destructive choice and maneuvering to maintain a fiction evolves from a lack of self-understanding, unwillingness to recognize the needs of the other person, and an inability to communicate what you really want. As a result, you are likely to pursue unavailable partners, a common form of self-destructiveness motivated by adolescent daydreams. Here is an example:

A middle-aged man was pursuing a woman who told him that although she was separated from her husband, she really wanted a reconciliation. He continued, hoping that she would discover that he is a swell guy. I asked him about his adolescent fantasies: "My fantasy was to be a savior to the person I loved. A girl who was emotionally down, repressed, or hurt was a part of it. I would save or protect her. I would be more acceptable if she needed help." He was currently acting out his adolescent daydream of making this woman happy by showing his concern and generosity although she made it quite clear that her heart was with her husband.

Most people have very narrow ideas about the range of people they will accept as lovers. This is an example of the transference of early fantasies. They transfer emotional as well as physical expectations. When you expect a prospective partner to be depriving, ungiving, authoritarian, and so on, and meet someone who doesn't fit those expectations, you are likely to manipulate that person into being what you anticipate. This is a form of game-playing in social relationships. You become inflexible and do not accept others on their own terms. You make the other person an *object* whom you try to manipulate to meet your needs, even though those needs are self-defeating.

Maintaining false ideologies that you learned early in life is another example of the transference of attitudes from one situation to another. Among those that many people have difficulty relinquishing are: "You must get married"; "Unless you have children, your life is wasted"; "Divorce is a failure and a scandal"; "Marriage is a guarantee that you will never be lonely."

Children are subjected to all kinds of pressure to conform to their parents' attitudes and ideals, and many of them continue to bow to those pressures as adults. These false ideologies misrepresent the nature of reality. They create barriers to new experiences because they interfere with treating each situation separately. This results in your creating demands that others cannot meet. Try to identify these barriers to new relationships, verbalize them, track down their origins, and attempt to get rid of the self-destructive ones.

Lack of Self-awareness

Some people have no clear sense of their own unique identity.

Here is an example of a woman whose self-awareness was very limited and of the destructive effects that the limitation had on her personal relationships:

• I asked a woman who was unhappily married about her marital fantasies before marriage. She reported, "I wanted somebody to take care of me. I wanted to work with that person to make a life. I had no idea how." She also expected "somebody else would make the major decisions. He would be there emotionally when I needed him. He would wave the magic wand, shield me from the realities of the world. He would be my age—we'd do everything together, grow older together, always be together."

When she was younger, she did not get much support from either parent when she was scared or angry. "You just didn't talk about it, and it went away." She was not encouraged to develop a clear image of herself and had no clear identity when she married. She could not select a man to match her needs, values, and temperament. On the contrary, "I was always trying to be what my husband wanted. I have no goals."

After therapy, she was able to be happy with a man with definite ideas and the ability to carry them through whether she agreed or not, one who could express his feelings.

Lack of self-awareness can lead to self-destructive acts in more than human relations. Any decision, whether it has to do with selecting a career, creating or carrying out a plan for an employer, buying a house, and so on, must take into account your capacity to carry out the decision and whether it suits your temperament, experience, and ability. Therefore, any effort that you make to understand yourself, through reading, dynamic growth groups, exchanges with friends, or psychotherapy, is going to increase your effectiveness in every area of life!

You must also learn to live in the present. This means realizing that the feelings you have about yourself and the values you picked up and the picture of the world you developed when growing up are in many instances totally different from today's reality. You must learn that you are no longer vulnerable to the emotional and physical forces of other adults. Your attitudes and actions should reflect the fact that you can now move away from pain, fight back when attacked, and negotiate as equals for what you want. Not to accept this degree of competence is to condemn yourself to remembering (and maybe exaggerating) your helplessness as a child.

Preparing for a Split

If you think that the time has come to break up an unsatisfactory relationship, here are some things to think about to "psych you up."

• *Recognize when the other person has given up.* With improved sensitivity, it is possible to determine whether there are any signs of life in the relationship or if you and the other person are simply going through the motions.

• *Be willing to acknowledge failure.* If you have had many unsatisfying relationships, or a marriage that has failed, try not to take it as confirmation of personal unworthiness. Failure can be honorable, but false pride is self-destructive.

• *Overcome false values.* If the wedding invitations have gone out, your parents are finally satisfied that you are doing the right thing, and your friends are deliriously envious, could you possibly back out? Yes! It is your life, so do what is best for you.

• *Face the inevitable hurt.* Don't defer a separation because of the pain it will cause. That only prolongs the pain and prevents you and the other person from moving toward better relationships.

• *Don't believe that you can never have anything better.* This suggests weak self-esteem. However, if most aspects of this relationship seem to meet your requirements and you are still dissatisfied, you may need psychotherapy to overcome your inability to relate and enjoy life.

• *Overcome emotional dependency and fear of loneliness.* If you lack autonomy you are likely to hang on to impoverished or humiliating relationships because the thought of going it alone terrifies you. It is better to be alone, and test your courage and self-reliance, than to be in a negative relationship. If loneliness is unbearable, develop your autonomy. Perhaps the discomfort will motivate you either to improve your personality or to seek professional consultation.

• *Develop self-assertion*. You, like many people, may be very uncomfortable about saying to another person: "You are not good for me. For my own emotional welfare I must separate from you." This is part of the general problem of identity, knowing what you can legitimately expect for yourself, and looking out for your own welfare.

• *Forget false sentimentality*. Don't get caught up in what used to be. When you artificially re-create a former mood, the memory keeps you hanging on when reality tells you it's time to let go. Enjoy your memories, be kind to someone who once meant something to you, but live in the present.

• *Evaluate obligations*. Don't encumber yourself with imaginary obligations. Too many people feel that they owe the other person something, or that he/she will fall apart without them. Apart from what you owe yourself, many obligations exist only in your own mind. Engage in reciprocal relationships and don't let large emotional debts develop. If there is a real obligation, try to be more giving. Avoid one-sided relationships. In this way guilt feelings will not assail your good mood and keep you in undesirable situations.

• *Confront feelings of guilt*. You may be well aware that you have mistreated someone and feel that a parting would deny that person retribution or you the opportunity to make up for what you have done. Staying around won't help the situation; face up to your responsibility, make your apologies, and start a new slate with someone else.

How to Split With Least Pain

• *Clarify what you want out of life*. Leaving a relationship is a good occasion to review your needs and goals.

• *Determine what you can reasonably expect*. If your needs

are legitimate, then you can expect fulfillment with somebody new. If they are excessive, you must modify your goals to avoid continued frustration.

• *Clarify why you experienced stress or dissatisfaction.* If you are not sure, discuss this with a therapist, dispassionate outsider, or do some further reading toward understanding yourself and your relationships.

• *Improve your techniques for preserving relationships.* Avoid carrying self-destructive tendencies into the future.

• *Evaluate the rewards and problems of the relationship.* Are there sufficient reasons for you to hang on, or are you there because you have been kidding yourself or making unwise decisions.

• *State your intentions plainly.* It is dishonorable to simply disappear or to pretend that you will remain when you don't intend to. Give the other person a chance to express his or her feelings. You may learn something that will help you in your next relationship.

• *Don't rehash the whole relationship in great detail.* The mere fact of dissatisfaction, rejection, and parting is very painful. Avoid the possibility of a sordid scene and further pain all around.

• *Make a clean break.* The added phone calls and excuses to see the other person (leaving personal articles around so that the tie remains) are self-defeating. You will be sentenced to added months of suffering and to feeling as tall as the lower dimension of a snake.

• *Be prepared to suffer.* Nobody gives up a relationship without depression and a sense of loss. If it is a good decision, however, you will also have a sense of relief and freedom. Now, if you learned and grew through the former relationship, you can choose somebody else with a sense of optimism.

If you have had a series of poor relationships, or if certain aspects of your personality have proven to be self-destructive, you would probably benefit from professional consultation to speed up your personal growth.

Chapter 8

A Constructive Approach to Anger

Anger is an extremely complex emotion, which most people mishandle. You may have been taught to behave in accordance with a set of contradictory myths that bear no resemblance to the way people act in the real world. Let's look at some myths that can cause you to mishandle anger in important relationships.

Myths

- True love never runs smoothly.
- Anger is a sign of bad breeding; therefore, if you express it, nice people will reject you.
- Every disagreement has to be resolved; therefore, it is important to win arguments.
- Never take revenge.
- The best way to deal with an aggravating situation is to ignore the person who provoked it.
- Your obligations to your parents and other family members require that you accept abusive treatment.
- Express your anger immediately—restraining it is bad for your health.
- It doesn't matter what you say in anger because the other person knows that you don't really mean it.

When you read this list and detect the contradictions, you will realize that one of the reasons it is so difficult to resolve conflict is that anger has different meanings in different situations. Furthermore, when you become angry and react violently or bottle up the anger, this itself is a link in the chain attaching one event to the next.

Extremes of Expressing Anger

Consider some of the effects of *withholding* anger:

• "My outbursts were provoked by my inability to get a response." (The partner's ignoring the mutual anger and conflict only made the situation worse.)

• "I would get involved with men who didn't lose their temper. I thought I could get them to express anger. I found even-tempered men dull. I like some excitement." (Ignoring the antagonism of this woman only provoked resentment and boredom.)

• "I came from a family that fought all the time. I knew after three weeks that my marriage was no good, but it took me twelve years to get angry. Divorce meant failure to me." (Keeping her dissatisfaction quiet wasted some of the best years of her life.)

Holding back anger was unsuccessful in achieving emotional fulfillment, although it had different meanings in each incident.

Now consider the effect of *hostile* outbursts:

• "To be skilled at arguing is very destructive. My husband has an explosive temperament. He is a bundle of complexes. He was always stepping on nerves. I knew he had a volatile temper from what I had heard about his first marriage, but I felt he would change. He probably felt justified after the breakup of his second marriage. He was absolutely self-justifying." (This man didn't learn from experience how destructive his anger was in his relationships.)

• "I have trouble protecting myself without losing my temper. I am not calm in asserting myself." (Outbursts of anger, even when provoked, are not necessarily the best road to survival.)

• "My relationship with this man varies between a struggle for power and tenderness. There is a lack of dignity. I love him, but love doesn't conquer all. We both have anger, which we show in a struggle for power." (Anger can fuel hostile or competitive situations.)

Expressing anger does not solve anything. While there is no simple prescription for when and how to express anger, learning more about the feelings behind it can help you evolve some sensible approaches.

Our minds and bodies have really been constructed for survival under primitive, prehistoric circumstances. As relatively recently as 50,000 years ago, the tempo of civilization began to increase, and it was only 10,000 years ago that human beings began to occupy permanent dwellings in villages and the whole structure of human existence began to change. We were no longer reacting to the natural world but were forced to live and work in an artificial environment.

Our social/material world has changed so rapidly that there has not been sufficient time for evolution to breed the kind of human being who can flourish under the new conditions. Our minds, glands, reaction patterns, and emotions, which were bred for a primitive existence, are confronted with the emotional, social, and legal qualities of modern life. Anger and fear were originally emotional responses to realistic dangers. When our prehistoric ancestors' turf, mates, food, or possessions were threatened, they needed violence to drive off the aggressor. If this was impossible, fear drove them over the next hill!

This, of course, is an oversimplification. It was not their bodies alone that enabled early man to survive. The human being competed poorly with tough beasts. We have no horns, claws, hide, or shell, and we don't even run very fast. Our senses are not the keenest, either. Worse, since we have become quite large, we have to eat a lot. People are by nature voracious.

Our species survived by perfecting its ability to be dangerous! We assumed an upright posture, developed fingers, and evolved a big brain. These qualities were "selected" in our ancestors because they enabled them to invent, manufacture, and learn the use of better weapons. By this means we not only destroyed and utilized big beasts but also decimated competing bands of more or less related creatures.

This built-in conflict between creativeness-cooperation and destructiveness is a problem that each of us must solve individually. It is important, however, to recognize that many inappropriate feelings intrude on your present-day reactions to stressful situations. When you are angry you are probably unaware that ideas, feelings, memories, conditioning, and innate reactions are all mixed up together.

This sets the stage for understanding how irrational anger usually is. You have to learn how to make anger a constructive part of your life, rather than permit it to destroy good relationships.

The first step in handling anger constructively is to understand that you may not be discriminating between what is actually dangerous and what has only a superficial resemblance to a dangerous situation. Are you really being threatened or abused by somebody who bears you ill will?

Owning Up to Your Own Anger

Many of you have been conditioned to avoid expressing or even feeling anger. When you are afraid of expressing anger, you make all kinds of adjustments in your emotional life to avoid becoming angry. One person reported, "I interpret a gash as a scratch to avoid having to be angry." Perhaps you identify with this reaction: "I hold back and go on the defensive. I become apologetic and avoid confrontations." Another hazard of holding back anger is that you become very tense and thus overly sensitive to criticism: "I tend to have difficulty in handling anger. I react badly and withdraw when somebody starts criticizing me." These self-descriptions were all expressed by singles who felt that their anger hampered their ability to form satisfactory social relationships.

People who don't protect themselves risk serious psychic damage because they permit themselves to be humiliated. Since they feel vulnerable and "have small egos," they hold back their feelings and identity to avoid arousing anybody's anger or disagreement. They become colorless people who melt into the crowd, and isolate themselves from more outgoing, self-confident people. And even if they do make contact with assertive people, their passivity and vulnerability often make their companions uncomfortable. They are such tempting targets on which to displace hostility and at the same time such sensitive creatures in need of protection. Neither image is very appealing because most people feel more comfortable with companions who can protect themselves, thus relieving them of the total responsibility for controlling their own anger.

Hidden Anger

Are you one of those people who have nothing good to say about people? When something goes wrong, are you immediately critical? Are you considered extraordinarily hard to please? These characteristics may be due to secret or forgotten frustrations, perhaps early emotional deprivation. You may have been separated from one or both parents temporarily or permanently when you were young. You may have felt that there were too many other children. Perhaps one of your parents was indifferent.

Somebody who has suffered emotional deprivation frequently cannot accept the world as it is. Nothing is good enough, and only an extraordinarily generous or pathologically self-sacrificing person will not be turned off by the spongelike attitude that *nothing is ever enough*. In this way, anger that developed from early emotional frustration can contribute a lifelong barrier to forming good relationships.

Critical attitudes are another example of transference. The model runs something like this: "My parents always criticized me. Whatever I did was wrong. The only kind of emotional life I knew was a barrage of unaccepting, hostile, negative feelings. After a while, I learned to protect myself by replying in kind. I learned to expect all people to be hostile. Unconsciously, I respond provocatively where it is unnecessary. I find it hard to recognize that people differ from each other; some are friendly, and some are as hostile as I am. I unwittingly surround myself with people who are angry with me because if they are not angry to begin with, I provoke them."

Any inappropriate feelings can be transferred. In the singles scene, as elsewhere, companions may turn irrational cumulative anger and frustrations against even the most friendly individual. It is a kind of emotional brutalization. Anyone subjected to that often enough either sensibly withdraws or becomes angry and passes along his or her own negative feelings. This is what the psychiatrist Wilhelm Reich called "emotional contagion."

When to Express Anger

The best time to express anger is as soon as you become aware of it. You may not always be immediately aware of your feelings. It sometimes takes a while to realize that you have been mistreated, particularly if the mistreatment is subtle. Don't suppress the anger on the premise that it is futile to express anger after the fact—better later than not at all. If a relationship is worthwhile, speak up when you've been hurt. That is the only way to determine whether the other person is responsive to your feelings. If he or she refuses to discuss the problem, then a genuine barrier exists to improving the relationship. The anger builds until it is intolerable and then a split becomes inevitable.

Keep in mind these guidelines *to using anger constructively:*
• Identify specifically what has made you angry.
• Make sure that you are expressing it to the appropriate person.

• Be sure the degree of anger is appropriate to the provocation.

• Get it off your chest as soon as possible and at a time when the other person is ready to listen.

Unreasoning, violent anger is a social barrier. Inability to express anger is also a barrier because it results in the withholding of valuable information that might help solidify relationships with others. Extreme vulnerability to others' anger creates fear, which also acts as a barrier to intimacy.

Think of handling anger in terms of the "Ouch Principle." When somebody steps on your toe, you say "ouch." Why not react in a similar way to other hurtful situations. Express your pain and indignation about what is happening. Find out if there has been a misunderstanding, or whether there is some willingness to explain or compromise. If you discover that the other person is indifferent to your feelings, move on. Immediately.

Chapter 9

Becoming a Winner

"Rejection depends on whether or not I see myself in a good light." This is a fine summary of the experience of most singles.

The same factors that create success in other vital areas will influence your social success. My goal is to help you to build up your self-confidence through liking yourself. Then you can approach people and situations with the sort of self-acceptance that will maximize the likelihood of meeting your goals and minimize the chance of not succeeding.

The keys to becoming a winner include taking initiative, becoming self-reliant, and learning how to feed yourself in time of adversity. There are great advantages in becoming self-reliant, in not having your identity and actions determined by the presence of a partner. The chief consequence is that you can easily avoid self-destructive relationships when you experience yourself as an autonomous, self-respecting person.

Recognizing Vulnerability

You have already seen how vulnerability contributes to becoming involved in self-destructive relationships. Recognizing these feelings within yourself is a significant step in overcoming them. Feelings of inadequacy, the expectation of rejection, and the fear of being overwhelmed are all warning signs.

Vulnerability generally evolves from bruising experiences, either as children or later on, that are beyond your ability to cope with. Feelings of inadequacy develop into an exquisite sensitivity to pain. The chief way of overcoming them is by stage-managing your life to have more positive experiences and associates. I cannot repeat too often: Eliminate negative people from your life!

Develop Self-knowledge

A lot of singles who think that they know themselves really haven't the slightest insight concerning their true motives, needs, and attitudes toward the people around them. They live in a dream world, not listening to their feelings or recognizing their deprivations. They do not assess their goals and needs and then make decisions consistent with them.

The first step to being a winner is to know what you want to win. Without this knowledge, you cannot possibly build a suitable, satisfactory life. Understanding your needs and values can help you to select the kinds of personal rewards that make the difference between a mundane existence and a fulfilling, exciting one. You can be more selective in your companions when you are able to assess whether or not their goals and values are consistent with yours.

You must become aware of, and emphasize, your assets. Your positive experiences, strengths, social skills, and so on are part of what makes you attractive. You have to make these qualities available to the people around you if you want them to recognize your desirability.

You must also be aware of your liabilities, including the emotional barriers you create. You may ask, "Shouldn't I be accepted for what I am?" There are some qualities that are not subject to change—your basic physical characteristics, deeply felt ethnic and religious affiliations, and your temperament. On the other hand, there are many learned behavior patterns such as uncooperativeness, selfishness, hostility, suspicion, insensitivity, and so on that you owe it to yourself to unlearn.

You can achieve insight into what attracts people to you or drives them away by being aware of your own feelings and observing how others react to you. Train yourself to listen to the right kind of feedback. There are some people who can tell you objectively how you come across and offer advice on how to have more successful relationships and other experiences. Learn to recognize this type of genuinely helpful person. It takes inner steel to listen to criticism, but it is important to be open to it. (I am *not* recommending that you spend time with inherently negative people; although even they can sometimes offer accurate appraisals, they are often too destructive to be with.)

Develop Perspective

You cannot become a winner in personal relationships, or in other vital activities, without accurately appraising your strengths and weaknesses. Making these assessments is complicated by the fact that certain traits that may be valued in one situation are considered drawbacks in other situations. For example, compulsive punctuality may please your employer but drive your friends crazy. What you must do is determine which characteristics you cannot or do not choose to change, which are sufficiently flexible and to be changed because they are troublesome, and which are so destructive but resistant to change that they require some psychotherapeutic intervention. Here are some thoughts about developing perspective about yourself in the area of personal relationships:

• *Learn to see yourself clearly, recognizing your real accomplishments and contributions to others' welfare.* Stop transferring early negative experiences into today's life.

• *Learn to tell the difference between facts and opinions.* Stop treating other people's opinions as if they were absolute facts. One person's unqualified admiration would hardly convince you of your perfection, so why should someone else's disapproval make you feel worthless?

• *Learn that rejection does not wipe you out as a person.* Avoid desolation by building up personal resources that will enable you to feed yourself emotionally through thick and thin. Develop a circle of warm friends and nurture a positive self-image that can withstand those inevitable occasional blows.

• *Remember, you can't win them all.* Don't expect to be perfect, and don't be discouraged when you fall short of your goal now and then—just keep working at improving your average of wins over losses.

Eliminate the Negative

Never let yourself be degraded. If somebody with whom you have an ongoing relationship is consistently negative, have it out. Unless you can change the situation, get out of it. Don't let false pride keep you in a position where you are repeatedly hurt. To lose is not dishonorable. To stick around and accept humiliation is.

Many hostile, critical people really want to be stopped. They have underlying feelings of guilt and unconsciously seek punishment. They strike out maliciously against innocent people, with whom they have no real quarrel, in the hope that they will be punished for their provocative misdeeds. If you find yourself in that situation, strike back immediately, before you become a victim. Let the person know you are not a suitable target, and put yourself out of his or her range of attack. Don't subscribe to the adage that at bottom everybody is good, and you should look for the best in people. Unless there is some clear, consistent evidence of decency in a person, don't waste your time trying to uncover it.

Accept new people at face value. Don't be suspicious and guarded—but if you discover that someone has lied to you or tried to delude you, be very wary of giving that person another chance. There are too many sincere, worthwhile people around to waste time on phonies.

Don't lose in advance by assuming you're not going to get what you want. Go after what you want. There is nothing dishonorable about having somebody say no to you. The rejection may be that person's loss, the unfortunate result of his or her inadequacies. Think of each "No" as one step on the way to "Yes."

Recognize What Makes Others Uncomfortable

Competitiveness and constant demonstrations of your superiority will provoke people to avoid you or to treat you in a competitive or hostile way. You can recognize the tendency to inflate your own ego if you find yourself frequently putting others down or manipulating conversations to enhance your image at the expense of others' needs and interests. Learn to be sensitive to your own motives and how others react to you. Otherwise your efforts to be admired will only build social barriers. If you sense that you have a drive for superiority, there are some simple remedies:

- Learn to accept people for what they are.
- Leave room for others to have decent self-regard.
- Avoid snide or reproachful comments.
- Don't insist on having the last word.

Reducing Social Distance

It is possible to live in an emotional shell by seeming to be aloof, by not reciprocating others' warmth to you, by pretending disinterest, by becoming preoccupied with superficial activities, and so on. You might be doing this to avoid the possibility of rejection, or you might be playing the game of "hard to get" on the false assumption that it will increase your desirability. Be aware that anyone who responds with interest to that sort of behavior is frequently working out his or her own neurotic problems of rejection and would lose interest if you actually became available.

Problems of accepting warmth certainly can prevent others from drawing close to you and can prevent you from enjoying the fruits of a good relationship. Do you interfere with the goodwill of others by frequently telling yourself that the giver is insincere? Perhaps you have had close relationships that broke up unexpectedly, conditioning you to expect pain and to guard against the disappointment of having intimacy withdrawn.

Here is how one woman described her inability to accept warmth: "When there are signs of approval, I freeze up. I pull away when I am hugged—it reminds me of when I was a chubby kid and people used to pinch my cheeks. I can't accept encouragement except from somebody with whom I have a strong emotional bond. I'm afraid to give up part of me that rejects warm people. I set up barriers and criticism. The sick part of me accepts the criticism."

The inability to express warmth is sometimes a result of being cruelly treated as a child. More often it is the outcome of parental training that stresses the importance of maintaining a cool, polished, and poised demeanor in all social interactions. This sort of studied behavior can inhibit your responsiveness and intimidate the people with whom you come in contact.

If you really feel emotionally frozen, these barriers may have to be dealt with professionally by group or individual psychotherapy. But for many people, all that's required to dissolve that emotional block is a willingness to take a few risks. You have nothing to lose but your feelings of emotional deprivation.

Explore Your Motivations

As you make new contacts, go to work, spend your free hours, and so on, focus on what is important to you. Consider how you can fulfill your needs. Then do it. Are there trivial people and activities that devour your time and morale? If someone is making unnecessary demands on your time, your spirits, your money, your energy, your you-name-it, don't hesitate to put your needs first. Spend time with people who are important to you. Go to places you value or where you will make enjoyable contacts. If you've set aside a day or an evening for a particular chore, do it! Don't be sidetracked. Be self-disciplined. If you want a better social life, filled with more varied and interesting people, don't waste your time on trivia. Get out there where the action is.

Develop Alternative Resources

Realize that some totally personal, private resources are necessary for emotional well-being. You can't rely entirely on outside sources for fulfillment. Having some valued activity will take the sting out of a temporary setback. One woman took a rejection in stride because after many years she had developed the motivation to write a novel. Other people gain solace from or lose themselves in reading, music, the theater, various hobbies, or sports.

People who have no means of emotional support except the generosity of others are dangerously dependent. Sooner or later, their supplies run out. They have no one to feed them. They have not learned to feed themselves. Don't let that happen to you. Don't be in a position to say: "I don't trust my resources."

Chapter 10

Improving Communications and Openness

You can avoid a lot of misery by honing your communications skills as well as by making the effort to understand clearly what other people tell you. Better communications can either improve existing relationships or provide information to help you and prospective partners to decide rapidly whether there is a potential for intimacy. You avoid wasting precious time as well as unnecessary disappointments and conflicts, which, in turn, helps you to avoid becoming cynical and pessimistic.

Why wait months and years before revealing your basic attitudes to someone close to you? Why build up hopes and commitments that are bound to be crushed when the truth comes out?

There are two kinds of communication—open and manipulative. Open communication is clear, with no pertinent information willingly held back. Openness is the road to intimacy, which is what you are usually seeking in a relationship, and which has been described variously as:

- Expressing feeling without hurting the other person
- Avoiding the issue of dominance
- Being sensitive to the other person
- Feeling so comfortable you can say anything

• Being forgiving when the other person treads on your sensitivities
• Being mutually committed to the relationship
• Taking and giving criticism
• Not letting resentments fester

Of course, you may have encountered people who took advantage of your openness. There are people who will use information you give them for their own advantage and to your detriment. You have to learn to recognize manipulators—those who pretend to think or feel a particular way in order to conceal their real motives. Since acting on false or misleading information can be destructive, you have to strike some balance between being open and exercising prudence. If someone betrays your confidence, you owe it to yourself to make certain the behavior will not become a pattern if you permit that person to remain in your life.

Is your social sensitivity as sharp as it should be, or do you become too preoccupied with what you are thinking and the impression you are creating to be aware of the kind of people you are dealing with?

An important part of effective communication is understanding what is actually going back and forth between you and another person, and being aware particularly of your feelings and to what degree they are reflected in what you are saying and doing. You may detect that you are being used as an object to meet somebody else's needs or vice versa—either form of behavior is eventually self-defeating.

Saying You Are Angry Is OK

You may believe the myth that anger will drive away others. On the contrary, anger sometimes is the only honest communication. Of course, I am not encouraging sadomasochistic games, but rather the unavoidable expression of discomfort when any two people are around each other long enough. Here is an example: One of my patients, a woman who has been married about thirty years, has recently learned to be more expressive and reports that she is happier even though she and her husband argue more. She has learned the importance of expressing her own feelings. Her husband is a little surprised, but he is accepting, because now that she knows her own mind she has become more accepting, which gives him greater freedom.

Why Communicate?

If you want to talk so that you are heard, and to listen so that you understand, you have to know what communications are about.

Exchange of information. You want people to know who you are. This establishes your identity and gives others a basis for pursuing or avoiding a relationship with you.

Achieving your goals and needs. You give and receive information that is supposed to lead to action. At times you may not want to hear the message, or your partner may ignore what you are saying, but expressing clearly what you expect is, nevertheless, one of the most important skills in human relations. People who can't tell others what their needs are, are destined to be frustrated and isolated.

Letting others know your feelings. Feelings provide you with information about what is happening to you, and the expression of feelings has a definite social value. In expressing your feelings, you give information that affects your welfare; for example: Look out, I'm getting furious; help me, I'm needy; I want a mate, do you? Beyond this, because of social conditioning, expressing your feelings strengthens the bond between you and others. When you bottle up feelings out of fear of the consequences you leave yourself open to a wide variety of psychosomatic and emotional problems. Expressing your feelings not only influences others but provides emotional release for you.

Some people waste lots of time on irrelevant and trivial exchanges. The real meaning is: "I like you, I need company, I need a gimmick in order to have an excuse for us to get together." Unfortunately, the message seldom gets through, and all the small talk only hampers their efforts to overcome loneliness. On the other hand, being totally revealing in attempting to prove you are likable—warts and all—creates other problems. You can misuse candor by implying a type of false intimacy that misleads and may drive the other person away. Learning how to strike a balance between openness and reserve is a valuable social skill that can do wonders in opening up the lines of communication between you and others.

Barriers to Communication

Barriers to communication can be the fault of the speaker, the listener, or both. The following are problem areas that interfere with communications. Being aware of them can help you to communicate your personal wishes and needs more effectively, understand other people better, and recognize messages that are deliberately or accidentally vague or misleading.

FROM THE SPEAKER'S POINT OF VIEW

Self-preoccupation. Do you speak without being aware of whether or not you're holding the other person's attention? If that happens often it may be a tip that you are preoccupied with yourself and not truly making an effort to communicate. Listening and tuning in to nonverbal cues are as important to communication as talking is. Are you responsive to what others say to you, or do you wait impatiently to start talking again? Do you interrupt frequently? Do you really care about what the other person is saying, and whether or not he or she is listening to you? These are all important questions to ask yourself if you have doubts about how effectively you are communicating. It's possible, too, that the problem is not yours, but the other person's. You may be dealing with someone who is very egocentric, or not interested, in which case, why bother?

Nonverbal cues. Look for eye contact, facial expressions, and body language as well as verbal reactions. They can tell you a lot about whether or not you are reaching the other person. There may be someone around who is more important than you are, or your comments may come at a time when your listener is distracted. In these situations, efforts to communicate are futile and must be deferred.

False assumptions. Don't assume that everyone else shares your interests and knowledge. What fascinates you may be either boring or painful to the other person. Furthermore, it is easy to turn people off by using technical terms and unfamiliar abbreviations, referring to unknown third parties, and so on. It is simply basic good manners not to "go over the head" of your listeners. Communicate in basic English unless you establish that you are with somebody who enjoys sophisticated palaver. Make sure you are getting across.

Feedback. When you start to talk about something important, are you certain that the other person is receptive? If he or she is not in the mood to listen, you are exposing yourself to a needless frustration or antagonism. Be alert to feedback. Develop your social sensitivity. You may be having a profound effect without being aware of it. By ignoring the feelings you are stirring up, you can make a situation worse, create pain, destroy the possibility of starting a relationship or repairing one. Again, try to be aware of the nonverbal cues given by your listeners. Something may be going on that is more important than what is on your mind. If you disregard your effects on others, you are creating barriers to communication and inviting rejection.

Self-awareness. Knowing who you are, what you want, the kind of a person you are, who you want in your life, your goals, and so on will help you to communicate accurately with people. It will also enable you to relate to them in such a way that your social needs are met. Lack of self-awareness leads to misunderstandings and those "slips of the tongue" that reveal anger, frustrations, hidden motives, and fears in inappropriate ways. Hiding from yourself is self-destructive because it not only keeps you from achieving your goals, but also reveals parts of your personality that you may not want others to know about.

Verbal barriers. Even the most intuitive, giving, loving person cannot provide you with what you want without your asking for it. Unless you are presently surrounded by paragons of perception, you had better learn to talk clearly. Are you one of those people who creates verbal barriers by not finishing sentences? Do you let your voice trail off so that you cannot be understood? Do you punctuate your conversations with that invention of the Devil, "you know"? I know what? I know that you are careless or lazy or devious or dependent. That's what *I* know when you tell me that "you know." These verbal barriers are very conspicuous and are an invitation to others to mistrust or ignore you.

Preciseness. Get in the habit of speaking clearly and taking responsibility for what you say. Don't turn your mouth on until your brain is in gear. Ambiguous statements are irritating. When you say "He said," make sure that there can be only one "he." People have first names. When you say "I was anxious to do that," do you mean "eager" or do you mean that you would have "gone bananas" if you had been prevented from doing that? An important way of upgrading the quality of your social life is to upgrade your communications and see who is responsive to you and in what way.

Manipulative questioning. Making a statement in the guise of a question is often a veiled attempt to coerce the other person into agreeing with you. This invites a quarrel. The listener thinks that you are asking a question and gives his or her opinion. The result is usually surprise and irritation on both sides. No wonder, if what you really wanted was total agreement rather than another point of view.

FROM THE LISTENER'S POINT OF VIEW

Message altering. Do you distort what you hear, understand, remember, and then repeat the information, according to your personal biases and preconceived attitudes? Perhaps, for example, a friend of yours is always tastefully, elegantly dressed, but you perceive that person as being extravagantly dressed. Your feelings about that friend and money have altered the image to make it consistent with your preconceived ideas.

Feedback. Do you let the person talking to you know that you are not only listening but reacting to what he or she is saying? Don't be afraid to ask the person to repeat something you may not have understood, or to ask questions that indicate your interest in or disagreement with what is being said. The only message a passive listener communicates is indifference or boredom. If that's what you are conveying—out of shyness or uncertainty—concentrate on breaking through that feedback barrier.

Projection. Do you attribute your own feelings and attitudes to others? This is a way of not listening to what is said. You run the risk of mistakenly assuming things, possibly unpleasant, about other people. By ascribing to others your own anger, sexual drives, dependency, or attitudes of any kind, you block off communication and potential support.

Reality testing. Try to develop rules of evidence. Just believing that something is so doesn't make it so. By becoming more aware of your own feelings, and what stirs them up, you will be able to distinguish between your own motives and those of the people you deal with. People who are overly sensitive tend to misunderstand what is told to them. They see criticism and hostility where none exists. If you are not sure what somebody said to you, or are uncertain of its meaning, ask!

Acknowledgment. To improve closeness, it is important to let others know that you understand what they have expressed— whether it is love, anger, frustration, or whatever. Otherwise your relationships will be ambiguous. It is discouraging to others to feel they are not getting through to you about something important. Acknowledging what you have heard is an important step in coming to an understanding: The statement that you know what has been said, and you agree, is a firm foundation for further plans.

Guessing. I don't know why people are so reluctant to admit that they haven't understood what somebody has said. I myself have gone to the wrong restaurant, worked on the wrong assignment, didn't know what I had to do, and so on because I thought that I understood what was needed, or guessed that I did, but wasn't aware that *I didn't know.*

If you haven't heard, ask. If you aren't sure, ask. If you don't believe what you heard, ask. Repeat what has been told to you so that the speaker is committed to it.

Taking messages at face value. Frequently, a person says one thing but means another. The question "Will you dance?" says "Let's go on the dance floor," but it may mean "Will you marry me?" or "Do you want to go to bed with me?" or "Give me a chance to show my courage," or "Let me demonstrate to my friends what a gallant fellow I am." The hidden message can be the opposite of the open statement. For example, "I am asking you to dance" may imply that "you are the only woman around who doesn't have a partner." Or, "You can take me home" may hide "If you lay a finger on me I'll call the police." A tepid "I like you" may mean "you don't have enough money."

Many people have a hidden agenda of unstated or disguised intentions. For example, the hidden agenda for "Why don't I make supper for you before we go to the theater?" may be "I think he's a jerk. Let me see if he shovels peas in his mouth with his knife." Or, "Let's double-date with a friend of mine tonight" may mean "She has a wealthy boyfriend and we'll end up going to a fancy place." Perhaps "Let's go for a drive in the country" means "We'll never get back on time, so we'll shack up in that little motel."

You can't always read the other person's hidden agenda, but you owe it to yourself to be aware that it may exist, and to try to decipher it.

Hurdling the Barriers

The foregoing has outlined some of the various ways you may be actively or passively blocking communication. Exchanging

information in order to understand others is an important part of
openness and the establishment of firm relationships. On the way
you may find that there are important disagreements where you
thought none existed. In this way, you will spare yourself plenty
of heartache.

Single people frequently prevent themselves from exploring
new relationships and experiences because of preconceived attitudes. Remember: If your way of seeing things was perfect,
you probably would not be reading this book!

More About Hidden Messages

People communicate and relate to each other in a variety of
ways that are not specifically expressed in what they say. You can
do one thing, *say* something else, and *mean* something that isn't
implied by your words or actions. Attitudes are part of communication that can be hidden unless you and the person you're
dealing with seek them out. Some people conceal rather than
reveal their attitudes with words, and there are various ways you
may be influenced or manipulated by their hidden messages.

Dominant-submissive. The question of who will do whose
bidding is unambiguous when somebody immediately takes
charge and openly expects you to acquiesce to his or her wishes.
Sometimes, however, the message is hidden; you may find your
suggestions are solicited and then vetoed, and you end up doing
what the other person wants anyway. Dominance also can be
concealed in the guise of submissiveness by someone who asks
you to make all plans, and manipulates you into taking the responsibility and the initiative and also allows you to pick up the
bill. If you let yourself fall into that pattern you end up the slave
of the ostensibly submissive person.

Superiority-inferiority. This is different from dominant-submissive. In this area, people reveal who they think is *better*, not
who is *boss*. If you find yourself constantly being lectured to by
people who put down your opinions and make adverse compari-
sons between your education, job, friends, and experience in

life and theirs, you're letting yourself be drawn into the superiority game—on the losing side. Or you may find yourself in the reverse of that situation. Inferiority game players often reveal themselves by the halting, diffident pace of their speech, a barely audible voice, and such self-derogatory comments as, "Well, you really know better, but . . ." or "I really have no right to express an opinion, but . . ." or an exaggerated evaluation of what you have to contribute. I am not describing flattery, which is also an effort to manipulate, but the real feeling of inferiority that some people have.

Personal-impersonal. This is more subtle and can easily be misunderstood. Some people are truly interested in you and are deeply affected by your attitude toward them. Other people are professional charmers. They imply much more concern and affection than they deliver. You may not be able to distinguish between sincere and fraudulent interest immediately, but it won't take too long to determine whether their actions are consistent with their seeming concern. If their words and behavior don't jibe, your hopes for a close personal relationship are apt to be dashed.

Extrovert-introvert. People differ in the degree of interest they take in the world around them and/or in their own activities. Some are able to be highly involved in both external and internal matters. Others focus more on one area than the other. It is very important to evaluate a potential partner in these areas. An extrovert may form a very dependent relationship with you. Other people are important to the extrovert. Therefore, you must be charming, entertaining, reliable, active, and available. The introvert, on the other hand, whose own activities and interests are more important than interaction with people, may not want as close a relationship as you would like. However, introverts do have the power to form a few close, intense relationships.

Work-oriented/work-resistant. Since you frequently have to plan things with people—a picnic, party, community action, or whatever—a significant factor to be aware of in the people close to you is their capacity to remain goal-oriented and cooperative.

There are people who enjoy cooperative efforts or perhaps leadership. Others feel oppressed at the idea of working together with people or under somebody else's leadership. They joke, sabotage, or passively resist. Because so many activities are social, it is important to recognize the dimension of cooperation vs. resistance in people.

Closeness and distance. The distance between people when they stand and converse gives some indication of their relationship, although the preferred space varies with different cultures and ethnic groups. The physical distance people maintain is also a clue to the emotional distance they wish to establish between themselves and others. While you can't use this sort of body language as a definitive guide to someone's potential for closeness, it is something you should be aware of.

Sizing up others means using information gathered both by observation and by intuition. It requires a combination of objective and subjective evaluation. Add to that your growing self-awareness and you begin to have a sound basis for evaluating suitable relationships.

Chapter 11

Loneliness and Barriers to Intimacy

Probably the deepest craving that people have is for intimate relationships. By this I do not mean sexual experience, although this is frequently referred to as "intimate." After all, it is possible to have all kinds of sex play while letting your mind wander far away, fantasizing that you are with somebody else whom you know or imagine or would like to know.

If you are one of the people for whom life is incomplete without intimacy, it's essential for you to learn how to overcome barriers to achieving it. It is essential, too, to recognize those people who do not share this need, or who do not want intimacy with you.

Understanding Loneliness

Intimacy could be defined as the opposite of loneliness. It is not easily achieved because it means putting aside the defenses and shields with which you have surrounded yourself. Intimacy requires trust, fearlessness, concentration, and a willingness to give and accept emotional support.

When you cannot achieve intimacy, you suffer from loneliness, feeling emotionally isolated, uncared for, and deprived.

And you can feel isolated in the midst of people, surrounded by family, acquaintances, or colleagues. Frustration can be even greater when you want and expect emotional support and find that those you rely on are unable or unwilling to provide what you need. I know one woman who suffers from serious feelings of depression and loneliness. She comes from a very large family. One weekend when she was visiting her sister's family, the frustration was so great that she became dizzy and fainted. She wanted warmth desperately but did not find it in the midst of her relatives who were pursuing their own lives. In another extreme instance, a young man committed suicide by leaping from a window while his mother was in the room. She was by no means an unloving or otherwise terrible person. On the contrary, she seemed to be a normally expressive, interested mother. The point I am making is that the responsibility for overcoming loneliness comes from within yourself. The barriers to personal contact are self-constructed. You owe it to yourself to develop the courage and the social sensitivity to dissolve those barriers in order to experience emotional warmth and offer it to others.

Identifying Depression

Loneliness can be confused with depression. Even psychotherapists occasionally make this mistake. The reason is that one of the most significant causes of depression is the loss of somebody close to you—through death or the dissolution of a relationship. In those cases there are often complicated but temporary emotional reactions, including the frustration of not being able to settle unresolved problems with the departed, resentment at being abandoned, loss of status (for example, marriage or other affiliations) or self-esteem. Inevitably, when you lose someone precious, you are going to be lonely and depressed for a while because of the lack of emotional contact, support, and companionship.

Depression is a more persistent state, characterized by emotional pain, hopelessness, and helplessness. It makes you feel trapped and thus your energy output is hampered, so that work and play are difficult. Your appetite for food and sex may be reduced. Above all, when you are depressed you are almost constantly aware of the emotional pain of self-reproach, anger, and anxiety. This preoccupation with pain severely limits your capacity to form new relationships because it makes you indifferent to others and discourages others from approaching you. The resulting loneliness only intensifies the depression, and the pattern can easily become self-perpetuating unless you recognize it and make a conscious effort to alter it.

You should also be aware that there are a number of biologically caused (endogenous) depressions. These certainly interfere with social living but often can be properly treated medically. True loneliness is different from socially derived (exogenous) depressions. There is a feeling of emptiness and isolation. One significant difference between depression and loneliness can help you to decide which of these conditions you may be suffering from. Of course, they can also coexist. When you are depressed, frequently you are having a relationship in your mind with the image or fantasy of the lost one. You remind yourself of the good times and the bad, what you said, wanted to say, or should have said. You imagine new experiences, change the endings of old ones, and generally maintain an imaginary relationship with a real person.

When you are lonely, you can also have an active fantasy life, but the quality is different because your fantasies usually involve the creation of idealized people. The content of your daydreams, therefore, is totally imaginary and very pliable. When you are depressed you generally are directing but not expressing your feelings of anger toward a real but unavailable person. Lonely people have no specific individuals to focus their fantasies on, and their daydreams tend to be a form of wish fulfillment.

What is the origin of the pervasive and self-destructive feelings of loneliness and depression? What purpose can they serve? Why do you experience such pangs when deprived of something that is only emotional in nature?

Why We Need People

The need for people is probably built into the nervous system. Humans come from a line of ancestors who had to band together because they were too weak individually to survive against the elements and predators. The individual who did not feel the need to be allied with the band, or who was excluded for some reason, had little likelihood of surviving and passing along his or her genes. The need for others, social skills, cooperativeness, and altruism may all be hereditary qualities.

Humans are born completely dependent, and have a long period of conditioning during which they learn how to get along with their families and are extremely vulnerable to parental and peer attitudes. The reactions of others, particularly parents, are crucial to children, and many people carry this dependency into adulthood.

Therefore, a genetic capacity aimed at survival within the family, combined with a long period of dependency and vulnerability, conditions many of you to believe that unless you are receiving constant emotional support you are in serious trouble.

Barriers to Intimacy

ANXIETY

The capacity to enjoy intimacy is developed—and can be ruined—within the family and through other early social experiences. Children are not born with strong psychological defenses against mistreatment. They develop constructive attitudes only if their parents are sensitive to what they feel, help them to understand their emotions, and then respond in a loving or helpful way. Children are very aware of mixed messages of acceptance and disapproval—messages of insincerity or ambivalence. If as a child you felt that your emotions were considered important and valid, you learned trust and how to be intimate. If you felt mistreated, or that what you expressed either was not taken seriously or was criticized, you no doubt learned to be defensive and began to feel alienated.

The way you were treated by your parents, brothers, sisters, neighbors (both adults and children), teachers, and other relatives taught you to anticipate how you would be received by new people in later life. Because of those early experiences some people can achieve close ties only with potential sexual partners, others only with members of the same sex, still others only with people in some way not their equals. Some people can be close to children or pets but not to adults. Others develop an acute fear of intimacy because it is associated with being trapped in unhappy situations in which their feelings are stepped on or ignored.

Perhaps an extreme example of long-lasting fearfulness is a woman client of mine who told me that when she was young her father wanted her to play with him sexually. She told her mother, who said she didn't believe her. What seems more likely is that her mother actually did believe her but ignored her daughter's complaint because she did not want to or feel able to do anything about it. This led the girl to conclude (not irrationally) that her parents were in conspiracy against her. Because the mind does not readily erase information of an emotional nature, she has maintained a deeply suspicious attitude that manifests itself in paranoid ideas about the people she sees on the street and on buses and trains.

In a sense, we are all somewhat paranoid—often fearful of unfamiliar people and situations. Yet life is jarring, and these fears are frequently enough justified. We set up barriers to intimacy and thus contribute to the already high level of emotional pollution in our social atmosphere.

Skepticism, pessimism, and disappointment prevent you from accumulating new experiences that could reeducate you as to your real value. Low self-esteem is maintained, which interferes with your capacity for intimacy. When you believe that nobody can be trusted, your entrance into a relationship is very risky because you expect rejection. You may even believe that to be treated well is a temptation, a trap, or a tease! You then set up all kinds of barriers to test the other party's sincerity. This self-destructive game playing arouses hostility and invites genuine rejection.

SELF-HATRED

Low self-esteem limits the possibility of achieving companionship and intimacy. What we tell ourselves can have the effect of keeping us lonely.

"I am rotten. Therefore, I cannot compete, participate in activities, or ask for any consideration. If I do these things, I will be rejected and reminded how terrible I am. I sometimes don't even dare think about myself, because this, too, will remind me of how rotten I am."

As a result of hanging on to old feelings of inadequacy, you ignore new information and deny your capacity for growth and change. You shield yourself from new, constructive experiences, as well as from positive thoughts about yourself and your achievements. You continue to ruminate about how rotten you are and what a terrible world this is.

GIVING AND TAKING

An intimate relationship involves an open exchange of feelings, thoughts, and actions. If giving is important, so is taking. For many people taking confirms their own feelings of weakness. Compulsive givers often are giving not out of generosity or offering something that others want. They believe that the gift of food, money, or whatever is their passport to happiness, and are deeply disappointed when their gifts are not appreciated.

Conversely, the compulsive taker is equally unappealing. If you sense that you have something of this in you, if you tend to measure all relationships in terms of what you *get* from them, try looking at those relationships another way. Find out what you *give* to them and whether your output is enough to sustain another's realistic needs.

Barriers to intimacy are revealed by attitudes such as these:
- "I'm afraid to give up the part of me that rejects warm people."
- "I always consider others insincere until they prove themselves."
- "I don't think that I can have a good relationship."
- "Today, people are not interested in real contact."

Such attitudes indicate some degree of fear, but if they suggest caution, what about the following?
- "Marriage is too close a relationship. It corrodes the mind!"
- "It's dangerous to surround yourself with friends. You're missing the reality of the opposition."

These attitudes militate against forming emotional ties and are very difficult to overcome in others or in yourself. If you have these fears, yet want an intimate relationship, therapy may be necessary.

Why No Intimacy?

If you are troubled by the lack of intimacy in your life, explore your overt behavior and the attitudes behind it. Are you shutting out other people because you're afraid of revealing yourself by expressing your feelings? Do you shut them out by ignoring their feelings and assuming theirs and yours are identical? One method is as effective—and self-defeating—as the other.

One patient of mine grew up believing that everybody had the same thoughts. He had been part of a group that wore the same kind of clothes, talked the same language, went everywhere together, and generally followed the lead of one dominant person. Everyone conformed to the leader's attitudes and behavior.

Years later, when he was an adult, he and the woman he was involved with ended their long-standing relationship. Only then did they start to talk things over and become aware of important differences in their viewpoints. He realized he had never listened to her or even considered that she might have ideas and attitudes that were different from his. In group therapy he began to listen to others and to realize that different people see things differently. The realization came too late to save the previous relationship but nevertheless made it possible for him to develop more realistic and mutually rewarding relationships from that point on.

Another patient of mine believed that intimacy obligated him to talk about his failures. As he put it, "If you are cocksure, why be intimate. If you're strong, you don't need intimacy. Loving makes me feel weak and vulnerable, so I withdraw. I don't want to have to reveal how weak I feel. My father was a closed man. If he revealed his feelings, my mother would break his balls, or she would start complaining that her problems were so much worse than his."

You can anticipate some feeling of emotional relief if you can express your weaknesses and still be accepted. Yet, prudence suggests moving gradually with a new person, because premature and inappropriately revealing disclosures may drive him or her away. Proceeding toward intimacy at a reasonable pace is one way of determining how compatible you and the other person are and allows a sound relationship to develop.

Here is another example of how self-destructiveness interferes with intimacy. A man commented:

"We all have a sense of loneliness. Maybe I have to hang on to my loneliness. Maybe I have become involved in my loneliness. I doubt that I will find that special woman. I want security and love and acceptance. But if I met someone more secure than I am, it would heighten my own insecurity. I feel more secure with insecure people. I don't let women baby me."

This man avoids emotionally healthy women. Consequently, he denies himself the support and healthy encouragement that a stable, secure person could provide. He is really saying that he doesn't deserve very much and isolates himself from anyone who might elevate his spirits and improve the quality of his life.

Loneliness exists in marriages, too. One of my patients was married to an unloving man she no longer cared for. She complained that he acted more like a father than a husband. As a result, she began devoting all her energy to her job. She felt empty and frustrated by her husband's inability to be loving. Her solution was to have an affair with another man. She says that her present lover "gives to me continuously. I enjoy his body, touching and holding him like a doll. I don't enjoy sex with him as such. However, I get turned on physically out of my own self."

This woman's situation illustrates how complicated it is to experience intimacy. How can it be that her husband treated her like a daughter yet she felt unloved? Why is it that she enjoys her lover's body as she would a doll, yet isn't physically aroused by him. Although her husband had feelings for her and was a responsible man, he did not provide the kind of attention she wanted. And while she doesn't want to be treated like a child, she enjoys treating her lover like a doll. He doesn't even have to take responsibility for arousing her. She can experience intimacy only with someone who permits her to play out a role that she learned in coping with earlier frustrations. Early fantasies often direct one's later love life toward fulfillment or disaster.

Reducing Loneliness

Here's a summary of some down-to-earth guidelines for decreasing loneliness and improving your ability to achieve intimacy.

• Be active. Unwanted solitude often breeds self-pity. Staying home and bemoaning your fate only intensifies your emotional pain and sense of isolation. Increasing your contact with the world around you by engaging in activities that interest you will bolster your self-esteem. At the same time you will increase the possibility of meeting congenial companions with mutual interests.

• Be selective in your friends. Many lonely people seem to seek out others who are equally at a loss for companionship. For example, a lonely woman, Agnes, became friendly with a recently widowed woman. The widow, Betty, was afraid to travel about the city. Consequently, Agnes found herself spending all weekends in Betty's apartment. It didn't take long for Agnes to feel cramped, but she had not developed any interests that would allow her to become involved in activities where she could meet more lively companions. Agnes' experience underlines the need to find friends who will encourage broader horizons, not constrict yours. As a participant in one of my workshops commented, "Loneliness is a habit; two lonely people do not necessarily make a good match."

• Feed others. If new acquaintances feel that you are a clutcher, too fearful, or someone who narrows their horizons, they are likely to avoid you. When you find constructive people, meet them halfway, be open to their overtures, make it clear that you want companionship but don't overwhelm them with your need for them and do make it pleasant for them to be in your company. When your friends feel that you have something to offer them, your own life will be far richer.

• Feed yourself. Being alone is not the same as being lonely. Even if you have dozens of friends, and a spouse or a lover, there are times when you are going to be alone. Don't waste that time on feeling deprived when you can use it to give yourself emotional and intellectual nourishment. You can provide yourself with stimulating companionship via movies, books, TV, concerts, lectures, and so on.

• Develop activities that can be shared. A hobby is *not* the emotional equivalent of solitary confinement. Many activities, ranging from card playing to jogging, bring you into contact with other people. Other activities, such as my own great favorite, flower photography, may take you away from people for a while but yield a beautiful end product that others can enjoy along with you. An interesting hobby helps develop your autonomy and also gives you something to share with other people.

• Don't assume that a mate will solve your problems. The divorce courts and psychotherapists' offices are filled with people who made that mistake! You must be a whole person to enjoy a relationship. By having self-esteem, by being able to function alone, you put yourself in the position of viewing more objectively the qualities of a prospective partner. Be aware that when your emotional needs cloud your judgment you are vulnerable to the "any warm body" disease. If you succumb, you will find yourself as inadequate as before, with the added handicap of being paired off with the wrong person.

Chapter 12

Recognizing
Suitable Relationships

There are some definite qualities to search for in developing suitable relationships. It is an active process, more than merely avoiding people who will ultimately prove destructive to you. However, a previously good relationship can become self-destructive if there are disagreements that are not resolved properly.

A good relationship is one that takes into account the kind of a person you are. Your fantasies and ideals are not the most reliable guides to the right partner. Assess yourself. Answer the basic questions: "Who am I? What sort of person am I? What do I have to offer? What needs of mine are not fulfilled? In what way am I a unique person? What kind of person would enjoy a relationship with me?" Once you know the answers, you will be in a position to recognize a suitable relationship, to judge how well a particular person will fit into your life, and whether you can satisfy that person's needs.

Remember—you may be all wrong for one person but perfect for somebody else.

Be Honest With Yourself

In selecting a partner, you have to be receptive both to the ideas and feelings that are openly exchanged between you and to your own private reactions. If you refuse to recognize problems, and choose to disregard anything you hear and observe that doesn't agree with your preconceptions, you are asking for trouble. Learn from the experience of the woman who said: "Although it's painful, it's better to clarify early on that a person doesn't love you, because it hurts too much later to clear up the illusion that he does love you."

Another woman reported the following situation: "Philosophically I have a deep conviction that people change. It was nothing that we could discuss. He was opposed to psychoanalysis. Even hearing the word sent him into paroxysms of rage. We never discussed his temper. I idolized him as a person. It was a terrible flaw in a wonderful, truly concerned person."

Do not assume that change will take place unless the other party admits that something is wrong. This man was not upset by the results of his behavior. On the contrary, his partner let him get away with it, and it, consequently, continued.

You are inviting disaster by remaining in an unsuitable relationship—whether the reason is fear or compassion. Many people have told me of the problems that resulted when they felt unable to get out of a relationship or couldn't be truthful about not being physically attracted to the other person. Being dishonest with yourself or feeling an obligation to continue against your will creates resistance, frustration, and anger.

You can delude yourself into believing that everything will be all right once you get to know each other better. But in reality, significant disagreements probably won't change. They may be temporarily masked and then become the basis for conflicts later on. As one of my patients acknowledged when talking about the end of a love affair, "Clarification would have brought it to an end sooner. The gulf was too great, although we did love each other very much."

When you want somebody, it is very tempting to camouflage the true facts about yourself, deny what is being told to you, or tolerate barriers to the exchange of information. Humor and changing the subject are great for evasion.

Availability

Availability must be considered after you have satisfied your-self that openness and trust exists. The willingness to be com-mitted varies with a person's stage of life and frame of mind. Do not assume that the other person's needs and intentions are the same as yours. Some people refuse to become committed.

Many people pretend to become involved but, for neurotic reasons, cannot form commitments. It would be better if they restricted their interpersonal contacts to tennis or chess, but unfortunately they don't, so you cannot always avoid painful experiences with people who can only pretend to be real and involved.

People offer a number of reasons to explain their refusal to be committed:

- I don't want to give up my freedom.
- I have a lot of growing to do.
- I need a few more years to make up my mind about you.
- To get close to somebody is to be out of control.
- I feel trapped—like being a helpless child again.

You have probably heard many of them already, and some of the following excuses that conceal a basic unavailability for in-volvement in a serious relationship.

- I want to keep cool for business reasons.
- I am taking care of my parents.
- I am continuing my education.
- My analyst tells me that I am not ready.

One man realized after his third date with a woman that he was getting nowhere. They were still shaking hands and when he asked why, her reply was, "You're a handshake fellow!" She was, in short, unavailable (to him).

Preconditions are also a sign of a lack of availability, though they are hard to avoid. The qualifications you establish for a potential mate are so ingrained by parental training and values, cultural norms, and peer group pressure that it is difficult to judge a new person on his or her real merits. For your part, you should try to overcome rigid stereotypes. On the other hand, if you have an indication that you don't match somebody else's key precondition(s), there is only one thing to do: Get dressed, go home, and find somebody else. *Immediately!* Among the preconditions some folks focus on are money, proper religion or ethnic group, age, education, politics, physical appearance, occupation, and so on. The list can be extended. *Do not swim against the tide.*

It is possible to be taken in by certain kinds of people who specialize in charm—perpetually sweet, smiling, and gracious to everyone. When you are emotionally hungry, or inexperienced in the ways of the world, you can mistake polish for genuine warmth. Learning to recognize that somebody is or is not interested in you personally can save heartache. Unless impersonal charm is enough for you, being involved with a detached person is frustrating because you can never have true intimacy with him or her.

Some people are reluctant to give up unsuitable relationships even when they know that the other person is unavailable. I recently spoke to a woman who told me that she was having an idyllic romance. Gradually it evolved that her partner was married, a highly religious man, and was beginning to develop qualms about their affair. She had tried to reassure him, but was able to say to me: "I know that it is going to end in disaster."

Game Playing

One of the most devious ways of concealing unavailability (from yourself as well as others), under the guise of intense participation, is acting out conscious and unconscious fantasies. These life scripts can begin in adolescence or earlier and can influence your sexual (and other) relationships throughout life. What happens is this: As children or adolescents most of us developed daydreams in which we and fantasized persons played idealized parts. These daydreams often occur in response to feelings of helplessness or frustration. We believe then that the imaginary events will solve our emotional problems if they come to pass. It is important to remember that the emotional conditions that determined these childhood fantasies are no longer actual factors in your adult life. And to continue acting out variations of those early fantasies is as self-defeating as using an out-of-date map.

The people you try to manipulate into playing supporting roles not only don't know your secret scenario, but generally wouldn't want to act in it if they did.

The unconscious motive for such manipulation is frequently the compulsive need to seek redress for past humiliations inflicted by parents or siblings. The paradox is that in acting out these scripts you often overlook or reject the very people who are responsive to you. Because your hidden goals are to reproach or punish those who hurt you and to compensate for prior rejection with the unqualified devotion of a fantasy lover, the reality of a relationship is irrelevant to you. On the contrary, if you identify a potential partner as being similar to a rejecting parent, you may enjoy the opportunity of displacing your anger and humiliating this inappropriate target of your hostility. Many tumultuous, apparently promising relationships end in hostility and perplexity because you or the other person was actually involved in continuing an adolescent struggle with imaginary enemies. To avoid being either the embittered playwright or the perplexed actor, you must be careful to separate your actual feelings toward people in your life today from the unresolved feelings you carry as a burden from the past. You should also try to be aware of whether the other person's behavior is appropriate to reality.

Bearing Grudges

Don't waste your time and energy feeling resentful about real or imagined grievances of the past. When you carry around long-standing hatreds, you tend to take them out on people in your life *now* for harm done to you years ago, often by people who are no longer in your life. One excruciatingly lonely man I know harbors resentment for rejections he encountered twenty years ago. He goes on being angry with people who might be good friends of his today if he let them. Gradually, I am helping him to live in the present and to stop trying to get even with adversaries of the past.

It is possible to change those patterns, as one woman confirms in her comments about becoming more responsive to the living present: "Lately I've learned to hear praise. I had to work at actually hearing when people validated me. I used to pull away. Now I enjoy it. God knows what they could have expected from me. When I contradicted the validation, it was the voice of my mother. It was as though a third party was in the room." She is giving up the influence of the memory of her mother's attitude and can begin to respond appropriately to people who like her.

Goodwill

Acceptance and good feelings are another sign of suitable relationships. The final outcome of relating to somebody who does not really like you is revealed in one man's sad comment: "I eventually asked for the divorce. I didn't want to wake up to those rejecting eyes." It is likely that the signs of dislike could have been seen even before the bargain was sealed.

Acceptance and openness are closely allied. When you can express your feelings without being hampered or censored, and accept what the other person has to say, assuming that neither of you is destructive, it is a sign that the relationship is close. Even criticism, expressed reasonably, can be an expression of concern. It can give you information to use toward changing undesirable personality traits, help you understand the necessity for compromise, or correct misapprehensions about what is really happening. While it is painful to hear criticism, it is important to train yourself to hear what significant people feel about you. Equally important, you must feel free to express your feelings—negative as well as positive.

One of the most persistent myths about human relationships

is that love and good feelings are mutually exclusive. Some conflict is inevitable, but the basic sign of a good relationship is consistent good feelings. Open discussion of problems keeps resentments from bubbling over. Good relationships are high in trust and low in reproachfulness, ("You didn't call me when you said you might"), selfishness ("Gimme, but don't expect anything in return"), uncompromising attitudes ("My way is the right way"), indifference ("You can hang around if you feel like it, but I've got other things on my mind"), and so forth.

Expectations

How much can you reasonably expect from one relationship? No matter how much any one person has to offer, it is unrealistic to believe that all of your emotional needs can be met by only one person.

People frequently do not develop the resources to feed themselves. Consequently, they place intolerable demands upon their closest friend or lover or become extremely depressed when no one is available. A suitable relationship is one that meets many of your emotional needs but does not prevent you from growing up! There ought to be a balance between the gift of warmth and the vise of overprotection. You don't want to continue making up someone else's emotional deficit or compensating for decades of frustration, and you can't expect anyone to want to do it for you. Furthermore, since people differ in their ability to be emotionally generous, their need for closeness, and their desire for intense experiences, a suitable relationship is one in which the level of exchange of feelings is mutually agreeable.

Occasionally two people with different degrees of interest in one another can be mutually gratified. You may be willing to offer love, whether or not it is returned in kind, so long as the other person is a willing recipient. However, when you crave a greater response than you receive (assuming that this is not a neurotic dependency), your emotional needs are not being fulfilled.

It is worth repeating that you must also learn to feed your-self. You can have all the sex, companionship, entertainment, and so on that you have the time, energy, and resources for and still remain emotionally frustrated to the point of depression. If you remain chronically emotionally deprived, despite what appear to be close and intense interactions with other people, psychotherapeutic intervention is indicated. Good relationships make life worthwhile, but they do not correct emotional disturbances.

Not all your particular needs must be fulfilled by a lover or close friends. Everybody needs some personal living space and time to pursue special interests. As you become aware of your own individuality, you can be sensitive to whether the people around you are encouraging your personal growth or hampering it.

Temperament

You reveal your temperament through a wide range of personality traits that particularly characterize you—the kind of energy you have, your typical moods, your ways of expressing feelings and handling other people's feelings, and so forth. When planning a move, you may decide that in order to avoid living in a mess, you will wait until the last minute to pack. Someone with a different temperament might choose to begin packing immediately to allow plenty of time for organizing things and labeling cartons so everything can be unpacked easily.

Recognizing the potential problems in a relationship with someone whose temperament is incompatible can help you avoid or at least anticipate tempestuous situations.

Among the other aspects of temperament to be considered are whether you are a "day person" or a "night person"; how intense your sexual drive is; what degree of physical activity you need; how high or low your anxiety level is and how you handle it, as well as many other qualities of mood, which create a lot of the flavor and "chemistry" of a relationship. Compatible temperaments are every bit as important as shared values, ideals, and attitudes. Too often when one person has a stolid disposition and the other has pronounced mood swings, or one is lighthearted and somewhat frivolous, while the other is serious, the two people find themselves intruding on each other's life space, being resented, and simultaneously resenting what is experienced as a lack of appropriate emotional response. On the other hand, sometimes the differences are complementary and create a welcome balance.

How you handle anger can have a decisive effect on the quality of a relationship. People who come from similar backgrounds often share the same ground rules for getting angry and showing it. Those raised in homes in which there was habitual violence, raised voices, and tension may tolerate extreme expressions of anger. The same behavior may be threatening and repellent to someone used to more restrained ways of expressing anger. Since anger, whether overt or hidden, involves intense emotions, any basic misunderstanding about it is very difficult to resolve. If you suspect that you and another person cannot deal comfortably with anger in relation to each other it is a good signal to split.

Money

A person's attitude toward money is also a factor in determining suitability. Money, like food, is frequently a substitute for years of emotional frustration. It can also be a symbol of status or the means to a preferred style of life. If you and a potential partner differ sharply in your attitudes toward money, the chances are that those differences will intensify with proximity. Don't ignore the problem, assuming it will resolve itself. Unless you can reach a viable compromise, your relationship is likely to be stormy.

Chapter 13

Action in the Singles Scene

Let's take a look at what goes on at some traditional meeting places. Keep in mind that if you do not handle the opening moves well, out of shyness or lack of skill, then nothing is likely to happen.

The singles scene need be no farther away than your living room. You, like many other people, may feel most comfortable meeting new people in your own home. Entertaining someone new at a party you've organized gives you a chance to see how that person fits into your world; it also gives him or her a sense of your life-style. A man I know whose obesity was a social deficit improved his social life by organizing a group rental of a house in a popular summer community on Fire Island. In getting the group together he had the opportunity to meet many men and women. "Inevitably I wound up with a girl friend. By the time all the arrangements were made and I started going out there, I knew dozens of women and some men also." Another man advertises his profession and the fact that he is looking for a secretary. This evolves into a party both for the women and for his male friends.

In looking over the singles scene I've reconnoitered a major museum, a famous singles bar, and a popular singles party. My observations may or may not surprise you.

The first thing I discovered was that there are as many couples as singles at museums, and that most of them were there to look at art—not to pick up someone.

Another thing I discovered was that lots of people are suspicious. About 50 percent of the people I approached with my tape recorder wouldn't even talk to me. Now, you may say that is a reasonable response to being accosted by a 6-foot 4½-inch man asking intimate questions, but I don't agree. People carry with them about the same degree of openness or caution wherever they go. There is certainly less emotional risk in answering anonymous questions than in forming new relationships. Therefore, if this relatively impersonal contact arouses distaste and fear, you can assume that many people you might want to be intimate with have pretty high barriers.

I also observed that a lot of people seem to have one-track minds. The most glaring examples were at a large singles party where the need to make out superceded all other considerations. Few people would take the time to answer questions, even though there were scores of people around and a few minutes lost would not have meant a ruined evening. This was particularly characteristic of some of the most attractive men, who were barely courteous in their refusals. I report this because it points up an axiom worth noting—that watching how somebody treats another person can give you a good idea of how that person will eventually treat you. Beware of the self-centered hedonists out there—they are poor risks if you're looking for commitment and intimacy.

I asked people what they expected when they went to the places where I interviewed them, what kind of social mistakes they observed, what kinds of people turned them on, what they thought was the secret of social success, and their reaction to being single.

The Metropolitan Museum of Art

As I noted earlier, I learned that most people go to museums to look at works of art, not to pick up someone or to be picked up.

My survey of twenty or so interesting-looking men and women wasn't scientific, but it was a practical sample that included a variety of physical types, ages, and backgrounds. The results were as follows:

MEN: None had come to socialize, two could be seduced into doing so.

WOMEN: None had come to socialize, one reported that she might be seduced into talking to a man.

It would seem, then, that museums are not ideal places for making new friends. You can try, but do not attribute lack of success to your own failings. Be open and pleasant, and if your friendly overtures are rebuffed, remember that the rejection comes from somebody who doesn't know you and has no significance in your life. Enjoy the paintings and sculpture around you, perhaps discover some new favorites, and don't count on expanding your social circle.

A Singles Bar

Probably the crudest, least cooperative group I met was at a well-known singles bar in New York City. When I asked one of the men what he expected to find at the bar, he replied: "A piece of ass. It works about half the time. I have to take the initiative most of the time. Any mistakes that can be made here? Getting VD. I haven't got it yet."

Another man made the following reply: "I love to rape. It's the greatest thing in the world. You find out the girl's address. You go up with a bullshit excuse and you rape her about ten times in a night." It's hard to know whether this was fantasy or fact; the comment was made in the presence of some other men he might have known and thought he could impress with his macho stance. Regardless, people like this contribute to an atmosphere of suspicion. Many women probably are raped or threatened without actual physical abuse into having sex. And the possibility of coercive sex makes a lot of women wary and defensive toward all men.

Here are some of the other comments elicited by my questions.

Male: "I expect to spend $15 to $20 for bar tabs and if we have dinner, $20 to $40. I think about pussy when I think of coming here. Body first and mind second. What kind of mistakes do I make? Being too cordial and not aggressive enough. You've got to be aggressive. If you see a chick you want to score with you have to put the make on her immediately and keep any other guy from moving in. You have to be possessive without her knowing that. The real secret of success is money. I am and have been and will be single for an unlimited amount of time and think it's great. Keep on fucking."

Female: "I expect the people I meet here to be friendly. I always wait until men approach me, but there are times when I'd like to light a fire under their behinds. They shouldn't stand around talking to each other and looking instead of making contact. I'm sick and tired of being single. The single scene is horrible! No, it's not horrible, it just has more minuses than pluses. The fact that people are not friendly is my biggest gripe. Everyone is uptight waiting for somebody else to make the first move. The best part of being single is the lack of responsibility. You can do whatever you want to do with your money—nobody tells you what to do or when to do it."

Male: "Girls approach me infrequently. How I feel about it depends on the girl. If I think that I'll like the girl I'm not uncomfortable. But if it's somebody that I really don't want to talk to, it makes me uncomfortable because I have to get out of it. You can tell a lot about a woman from the way she dresses and handles herself. Most of these people are trying to look like somebody they're not, and I can spot that right away."

Female: "I really don't expect anything at these places. I'm very cynical. I don't expect to meet the type of person I'd like to meet. I haven't been to a singles place for about two years. I come now and then out of curiosity."

One man complained that many of the women he met "come

on too strong. All they're interested in is money, money, money, and that makes me feel way out of my class. These women just want to go out and have money spent on them."

Another man commented that "every girl in New York City wants to play games. 'What do you do? Where do you come from? I don't know if I like you or not.' I feel I'm not allowed to express my real emotions. If I meet a chick I really dig and after one or two nights I say, 'I really like you,' she freaks out. She wants to know why. She's scared of it. She thinks I mean I want to take her to bed with me." Sincerity obviously is not a fool-proof way to overcome barriers to building a relationship.

At an Upper West Side bar that is more of a neighborhood hangout than a swingers bar, I talked with a woman who was having dinner with a friend. "I don't come here to socialize. I come here to be with friends. I have trouble getting rid of men sometimes. There were a couple of men bothering us before [which was why she was initially reluctant to be interviewed]. I would have to be desperate to approach a man. I resent it if a man looks at me as though I were a sexual object. If he looks at me as though I am a human being it's different. It's very hard to define."

Another woman had this to say, "Don't waste time with people who don't respond. I think women should start feeling that they come first. They should take care of themselves first—get what it is they really want. They would be a lot happier. Do what you really feel is right for you. Women always place themselves in relation to men. They are always performing for acceptance and love. It becomes a charade. You can't have an honest relationship if you're always performing for somebody. You have to be yourself, know what you want and go out and take it. I think too many people are afraid of having feelings and emotions because they are afraid of what the other person will think or how they will respond. There is a lot of phoniness. Singles bars are phony places to me."

I asked her how she spotted a phony. "You don't always know until you're in the middle of a relationship," she admitted. "He pretends he's always happy and accepting when all the while you're doing things that irritate him and he won't tell you. Then one day the whole thing blows sky high and he starts enumerating things from the past six months that he doesn't like. You can't always guard against it."

One man offered some insight into the phony behavior found in the bar scene: "A lot of girls seem to feel that going to a bar lowers their status. Some of them are very uptight about being in a bar, very defensive. A party is better for getting to know people."

When I asked people what sort of approaches they used or responded to, one man replied, "A girl should go up to a guy and start talking to him—try to avoid being hung up. She assumes in her mind that he's not the way he seems. He's some other person because he's at a bar. She should take an optimistic point of view. 'He looks like somebody I'd like to talk to and he may actually be.' She should go up to him, and if she makes a mistake, why should she care?"

Another man commented that, "People seem to need an excuse to talk to one another. Some of the excuses people use to meet each other are really novel. At first I thought your approach was a bad example, until you told me what you were going to do with the book. Even if it isn't so, you went to the trouble to think of a reason that would appeal to me."

I enjoyed the attitude of a young fellow who said, "I meet women in the street. I say, 'Hi' right there. It doesn't take courage. All you have to do is let yourself stay loose. If I see a really neat chick and do not go up to her, I lose face with myself."

Commercial Singles Party

What can you expect at a singles party? To quote one woman's comment, "I expect nothing. It's the middle of the week, and I have nothing to lose. I haven't anything particularly important to do. It doesn't interfere with my weekends." Another said, "It's interesting to see this rat-race scene. Not that I sneer at it, or that I'm above it in any way. You can't keep yourself out of circulation completely. It's a place to go to see people and talk. I expect nothing. I would go up to a man who is clean-cut, nice. You can tell that sort of person."

The men are more optimistic. "I'd expect to find somebody I'd be interested in seeing, somebody who is well built and good-looking—you know, the average individual."

The atmosphere was conducive to my asking how these people felt about being single. One man said that it was great. He had felt freer in the last three years than in the thirteen years of his marriage. According to one woman, "I love being single. It gives me the advantage of meeting new people, traveling, really enjoying life until I meet the right one and settle down. I haven't met the right one yet, so I don't know what he'll be like." Another woman commented: "It's a sad state of affairs being single." Still another woman said, "I think it's very sad if you get hung up about being single. I don't think you should just grab somebody for the sake of grabbing him. Just go ahead and enjoy yourself. Just expose yourself to people, keep talking, travel, meet a lot of people, that's how you enjoy yourself."

A man felt this way about the singles scene: "It's like getting into a crowd where everyone is trying to beat the other one out. I think most of us would really prefer meeting people on an individual basis, but that's not possible. Here you never get to know the person."

What are some of the mistakes people in the singles scene make? One woman was very kind. "There is no such thing as a mistake. What is a mistake to me wouldn't be a mistake to somebody else. To me, a mistake might be someone who is too pushy or comes out with a standard line." In one man's opinion, "The mistake is not being honest. People shouldn't pretend to be what they're not. Your good points will come out sooner or later." One man felt that it would be a mistake not to circulate. "That's my mistake, I'm talking to you." I told him that he was contributing to science. Another cynic said that he didn't really think that a mistake could be made at a place like this because "people are not really interested in what you say or do."

What attracts people to others? Most agreed that good conversation, personality, intelligence, looks, honesty, and a positive attitude were important factors. Others wanted sexual appeal at first glance, somebody to marry or at least go to bed with. One person commented that "the best way is to be natural, not to assume mannerisms, not to pretend an elegance or simplicity that you don't have. Just to be yourself is the key to social behavior anywhere. . . . The world is much better off in couples. I just broke off a relationship—it was a wonderful rest from the hunting scene. It was wonderful to do things together, but it's not horrible to be alone. I feel it's all right to be with myself, and if it's not all right to be with myself, nobody else will want to be with me."

My own observation was that virtually nobody enjoys the atmosphere of a big commercial singles party. This includes people who are perennial bachelors, male and female, and divorced persons who don't intend to remarry. They find it artificial, destructive, depressing, and generally time-wasting in terms of forming productive relationships. At the same time, many of them feel there is no reasonable alternative.

If you go to singles parties regularly, or even occasionally, there are certain basic rules you should follow for making the best use of your time and getting as much enjoyment as possible.

• *Be active.* Approach a wide variety of people and work on overcoming your apprehension about being rejected. No one is universally appealing, so everybody experiences rejection at some point. And when it comes from someone you don't even know and who means nothing to you, it doesn't have any importance.

• *Don't pretend.* Presenting a false façade sets the relationship up on the wrong foot immediately. Most people are quick to recognize phoniness and flee from it. And those who are taken in by subterfuge will only be disappointed and hostile when you don't live up to their expectations. Or if you try to maintain the façade, you end up trapped in a false identity.

• *Develop spontaneity*. Don't rely on a set pattern of conversational gambits. Instead, respond to the immediate situation. Ask questions to draw out the other person but don't interrogate. Be sensitive to areas the other person may want to share more fully with you or avoid entirely. Above all, avoid monopolizing, bragging, and putting people down. Hostile banter may appeal to certain types, but you have to consider whether or not you want the sort of contentious relationship that is likely to develop from that beginning.

• *Don't waste time*. If you meet someone you think you would like to know better, try to spend a little concentrated time alone with that person before making a date. Go off to a quiet corner and talk for a while. Fifteen or twenty minutes of conversation should give you a fairly accurate idea of whether or not you want to see more of that person. Nothing is gained by spending time with unsuitable people.

• *Take a positive approach*. Look for appealing characteristics in the people you meet—and let them know you've recognized them. Give people a buildup instead of a put-down, but keep it honest. Empty flattery will not attract any but the most superficial people, and they are not the ones you want to add to your life.

Chapter 14

Some Thoughts About Sex

Sex is experienced very differently by various people. Some people are indifferent to a lack of sexual activity for months or years but react passionately when the right person turns up. For others, sex is a strong urge detached from most other areas of life; their physical satisfaction has little or nothing to do with the specific partner. To still others, sex is an integral part of their life pattern and it is difficult or impossible for them to take on a sexual partner without establishing an all-consuming relationship.

Sexual need is often the greatest barrier to meaningful relationships between singles. Other types of emotional needs are more likely to provoke people to seek help or to try by themselves to overcome the problem. Among many single people, sex is detached from other considerations. How to get it—or how to avoid it—are their primary concerns. What they often do *not* ask is whether or not they need it, what role sexual experience plays in their lives, how sex adds or detracts from their personal goals, how they can change their sexual patterns in order to be more emotionally fulfilled, and so on.

Even those with healthy regard for themselves, who make efforts to achieve self-understanding and act accordingly, often have to cope with the distorted attitudes of others. Furthermore, standards of sexual success are largely determined by the norms of one's peer group. Since these standards may be foolhardy, dangerous, psychologically unsound, and in violation of your personality, it is important to establish a pattern of sexual behavior that is compatible with your needs and values.

Decide what is right for you based on your feelings rather than in the findings of the latest published sex survey or on pressure from your peers.

If there is disagreement between two people as to whether they should go to bed, there may be differences in other areas as well. And if one cajoles or coerces the other into sexual intimacy, the reluctant partner may have feelings of guilt and suffer emotional damage because of his or her unwilling acquiescence to a totally incompatible person. There really are no firm guidelines other than your own feelings about when or whether to have sex. Sexual experience may seal or sever a developing relationship. While physical intimacy will give you and your partner certain information about each other, it may also obscure other aspects of your personalities; it may solve some problems and create still others. You must know yourself and your potential. Don't be pressured into a situation that will make you feel guilty or uncomfortable.

The problem of sexual pacing indicates the degree to which sex is often divorced from any other personal considerations. One man complained that women seemed to expect him to make sexual advances whether they were receptive or not, leaving him to wonder, "Do I seduce them, take them home and say goodnight, or what? There's no way of getting to know the other person." When asked about her experiences, a recently divorced woman commented, "After my divorce I was fucking like a maniac with every man in sight. The men expected it. But why can't men and women be friends?"

If two people are sexually attracted to each other, why postpone sexual fulfillment until friendship develops?

Some people feel there is no good reason to wait. They want to explore all aspects of the relationship—including sex—immediately. Others experience the tension of knowing that the other person wants sex as a distraction and will, therefore, engage in sex even though they feel no personal urgency to do so.

Still other people feel guilty if they have sex immediately and worry about that the other person thinks of them. Not having sex also has profound effects. One woman felt that if she had been seeing a man for several weeks and there had been no sexual intimacy, and then the man stopped seeing her, she would have been devastated. To her this would mean a rejection of more valuable parts of her personality. She felt she could more easily accept his rejection if it occurred after they had had sex very early in their relationship. Some people rationalize rejection after a sexual experience by assuming that the other person has hang-ups about sex. And, of course, some men and women are interested only in one-night stands.

From the psychologist's point of view there are good reasons for two people not to rush into sex. Sex is an intense experience that brings the participants into a uniquely intimate physical relationship but often, because of the urgency to have sex, excludes the emotional intimacy that takes time to develop. As a result, after a premature sexual experience, the participants may feel a commitment or an obligation to people who are essentially strangers and with whom they seem to have no rapport. The personality clashes that surface may be irreconcilable and parting inevitable. On the other hand, many personality clashes could be avoided if two people approached the sensitive areas gradually, with growing knowledge of one another. They would have a better chance to learn each other's idiosyncracies and how to come to terms with them. With instant sex, the process of exploration is confined to one area. Other considerations, which would either encourage or discourage intimacy, are ignored, and the whole course of the relationship is determined prematurely by sexual impulsiveness.

The question of sexual exclusivity is frequently the focus of conflict in a relationship. No matter what the pressures, however, the decision to have an exclusive encounter or multiple sexual relationships can come only from an exploration of your own goals and needs. These are affected by prior experiences of intimacy and rejection and are determined by your history, the urgency of your sexual drive, the availability of sexual partners, and your expectations of the future. The person who has just left an unpleasant marriage or a long monogamous relationship may have no desire to find another exclusive partner. On the other hand, many people whose happy marriages ended with death of their mates want nothing more than to remarry.

One man commented, "I am not in a position to have a relationship with one woman but must have multiple relationships. I don't want to be dependent on one woman."

Another had this to say, "I am incapable of more than one relationship at a time. Since I was twelve I have been seeking one person to be dependent on me."

The first man's comment about avoiding dependency points out that multiple relationships serve a variety of purposes. Probably the most frequent unconscious reason is an unwillingness to become committed. A closely allied emotional stumbling block is the inability to be intimate. Both of these may stem from early experiences in which the child either felt emotional pain because of parental conflicts or developed a fear of being rejected by them.

The meaning that people attribute to sex will also determine whether they seek exclusive or multiple sexual relationships. Some people make a clear distinction between "physical" and "emotional" needs. To them, a "mere" physical experience is to be downgraded as lacking real meaning. Others do not distinguish between physical and emotional needs and are more likely to go along with their urges or feelings. Some people will go for a long time without sex if a particular quality is missing in the people they encounter. These individuals do not attach much importance to sexual desire as such. They seek a certain amount of commitment from both partners before they will indulge themselves.

If you are vulnerable to rejection or feel that sexual intimacy must be part of a deeper commitment, the issue of whether to become sexually involved early in a relationship has to be confronted every time a new potential partner comes on the scene. It is difficult to evaluate another person's intentions. This is so partly because you may be embarrassed to question the other person's motives. In sex the motivation to lie is very strong. It is also frequently true that people don't know their own minds. Finally, how can you predict the outcome of an experience before it begins. You or the other person may have every intention of splitting afterward, or of being loyal, when actual events cause you to change your mind.

An interesting change in the expected scenario was reported by one woman who started dating a known womanizer. His motto was: "No sex in three dates and I leave." She held out for several months. A good relationship developed. She felt that he wouldn't have seen her real qualities if they had had sex immediately.

On the other hand, people can know each other, have a comfortable sexual relationship, and not be bound by more than mild interest. Another woman related that even though she had sex twice a week with a particular man, they would introduce each other to new people because they were both interested in exploring other relationships.

This vignette is very significant. It illustrates that even a continuous relationship, which includes sex, may be insufficient to satisfy emotional hunger. Sometimes it is the inability of one or both partners to be giving. This can be remedied sometimes with a change of partners. However, it frequently happens that there are basic personality problems that can only be resolved by psychotherapy.

Sex is closely allied with all the other emotions. It can be an avenue for expressing or receiving almost any kind of feeling. Sometimes the need for affection becomes so great that you enter into relationships that are undesirable, even sordid, just because they provide opportunities to satisfy some emotional craving. Here is how one person expressed it: "My need for affection is such that I realize I'm blinded by everything else. I will take enormous amounts of abuse and humiliation from a man if he gives me the affection I need. It became clear to me that I sleep with many men, without sex, just to see if they are affectionate, and if they are not, I will not have sex with them. So, in essence, what I'm doing is having sex in return for affection. I am always looking for a certain kind of close touch and affection that I never experienced before with any other man. I met a man recently who was affectionate and warm in bed but detached and cool the next morning. It's still hard for me to digest that someone can be so warm at night and cool and detached the rest of the time. I tend to hold on, thinking, 'Why should I give up something as satisfying as the feeling that I can be one with another person for a whole night?' It's not so much the sex as the closeness. Sometimes I stay up most of the night, wishing the clock would stop. If there is such a thing as ecstasy, I feel it with him, and wonder if I will ever find it again with someone else. If that is all I get out of it, it's worth it to me. I'd rather hurt than not feel at all."

This attitude is typical of the reactions of many people who have emotionally empty lives. They undergo all kinds of negative experiences in order to get some affection. The value of what they receive, which becomes magnified in their minds, would not be acceptable to more emotionally fulfilled people.

In the good old, innocent days of my youth, unwanted pregnancy and venereal disease never happened to "nice" people. Today there is a more casual attitude toward these events. Abortions can now be obtained legally. This factor, together with the development of nonmechanical forms of birth control, has led to greater promiscuity and with it the spread of venereal disease, which is something every sexually active person has to take into consideration.

The symptoms of venereal disease are not always apparent, nor can you assume that your partner in a casual sexual encounter is necessarily responsible. You can guard against pregnancy, but have less control over VD, which is a strong argument for being reasonably selective about your sexual partners. You owe it to yourself to be aware of the consequences that promiscuity can have on your physical health as well as on your emotional well-being.

I suspect that some people miss good relationships because they have "tunnel vision." The easy access to sex hides many other qualities that a potential partner may have. The need for sexual novelty may keep you searching for greater degrees of excitement or variety rather than developing other resources within a relationship. Relationships have become like bottles—disposable. Today, everything is disposable, including people.

The foregoing has dealt only with *quantity* of sexual experience. *Quality* is, of course, also very important, so I would like to conclude this chapter with a few remarks concerning orgasm. On the surface it would appear that the experience of orgasm is the most important phase of sexual experience, the goal of the whole game. Whether you and your partner "did" or "didn't" becomes a measure of value of the experience, which is appropriate when the relationship has only one (sexual) dimension. Yet sex has many more components and can be a valued part of a relationship, even where orgasm does not occur regularly.

Let us start with a few facts about male sexual performance, or more precisely, nonperformance. Impotence is caused by more than the familiar psychological blocks such as anxiety. According to a study by Masters and Johnson, it can also be related to a wide variety of medical conditions, such as diabetes, multiple sclerosis, and even antidepressant drugs including certain tranquilizers. Nicotine can also hinder potency.

One of the ongoing controversies concerning female orgasm has to do with the nature and location of a woman's orgasm. It appears that the physiological response is identical regardless of the area that is stimulated (vagina, clitoris, breasts, or brain—if fantasy is brain-stimulation). Where women seem to differ among themselves is in their *preference* for vaginal or clitoral stimulation. While some sex clinicians assert that the *mechanism* of orgasm requires that the clitoris be directly or indirectly stimulated, interviews conducted by other investigators indicate that clitoral manipulation and actual penetration produce different orgasmic experiences. Many women report that their most intense orgasmic experiences come from masturbation—using either self-manipulation or mechanical devices. The next degree of erotic intensity is partner manipulation, and the lowest intensity occurs as a direct result of penetration. Considering these facts alone implies that there is no physical need for a sexual partner. However, investigations by Seymour Fisher * indicate that the following kinds of satisfactions were obtained by women during sex, in addition to the obviously erotic:

- Feelings of tenderness and love toward the sex partner
- Feelings of unique intimacy
- Satisfaction from nudity and display
- Enjoyment in being an object of admiration
- Satisfaction from being sexually competent
- Sensations of a unique kind of self-"release"
- Emphatic definition of one's sexual identity
- Fantasy and imaginative role playing
- Satisfaction related to the act of creation and reproduction
- Enjoyment of muscular and kinesthetic variations

Fisher speculates that women might "utilize intercourse" in the following additional ways:

- To reassure herself of her femininity
- To dispel her boredom
- To gain power over her sex partner
- To affirm her attractiveness
- To obtain unusual or even painful sensory experiences
- To find release from over-rigid self-control
- To be held and comforted

* Seymour Fisher, *The Female Orgasm* (New York: Basic Books, 1973).

There was very little evidence that particular psychological experiences—attitudes toward the mother, guilt, religious prohibitions, anxiety, and so on—which frequently are attributed as the cause of frigidity, were in any way connected with the orgasmic potential of this particular group of women. However, because the women in this study were all married, any individuals with strong barriers against intimacy or marriage were excluded.

There were two findings concerning the link between a woman's sexual response and her attitudes that are particularly significant.

In the first place, contrary to psychoanalytic speculations that vaginal orgasm is more mature than clitoral, a majority of these women rated clitoral stimulation as more important than vaginal stimulation as a source of pleasure. About one fifth felt that clitoral stimulation was absolutely essential to achieving orgasm. About two thirds would choose clitoral stimulation over vaginal stimulation if they had to make a choice. However, Fisher also notes, contrary to many assertions that the vagina is relatively insensitive, that the kinesthetic (essentially stretching) sensations women experience in the vagina are erotic.

Moreover, there are some psychological differences between women who prefer clitoral to vaginal stimulation. This follows from the fact that vaginal stimulation resulting from intercourse brings the bodies together in a more mutual experience. Clitoral stimulation can put the man in a position of being more psychologically detached, while the woman can be more of a receiver and the center of attention.

This relates to the next point made in Fisher's study—that the only psychological factor that seems to contribute to a woman having problems with orgasm was having experienced her father as being distant and detached. Most emotional problems do not seem to interfere significantly with a woman's capacity to experience orgasm, though it is likely that perceiving her sexual partner as unreliable might cause a woman with this background to be less responsive than her true potential.

What is clear is that no single prescription can make a person a good lover. Each new partner is a new experience and only through mutual alertness to each other's needs can you hope to achieve maximum pleasure. Through awareness of this you can learn to recognize exploitative sexual partners and rid yourself of them quickly.

Chapter 15

Beginning a Relationship

The very way you begin a relationship tells the other person—if he or she is shrewd—a great deal about what is going to happen. You present a kind of scenario for approval. You hope that it will be desirable and that your *person* and *role* will be acceptable. At this point, of course, you may unconsciously reveal more aspects of your attitudes and behavior than you really intend.

How Much to Say?

You can usually judge the openness and honesty of people by the similarity between the picture they present of themselves at the beginning of a relationship and what happens later on. As for yourself, you must choose how much you wish to reveal at the beginning. Some people feel that a preplanned conversational gambit is necessary to get them past their initial shyness. The trouble is that as actor or audience you may not distinguish between a helpful device that provides social courage and the giving of a false impression concerning personality, character, interests, and so on.

One of the chief fears is offering too much information in the area of what you consider your social deficits. For example, since such a large proportion of marriages end in divorce today, many people are separated with dependent children. Should you reveal this at the opening moments of a relationship? If this is experienced as a genuine barrier by you or the other person, it may be better to reveal it and find out whether the other person remains interested. What is the result of a delay? If you do delay, you give the relationship a chance to start, and perhaps there will be enough attraction for a firm bond. If you are genuinely interested in a relationship, and the other person later rejects you for this reason, then you have not only wasted time, but also exposed yourself to the humiliation of being rejected by somebody who already knows you.

Another possible result of the opening "moves" of a relationship is getting stuck in a particular position. You present yourself as assertive or passive, a giver or a taker, serious or lighthearted. You may set up expectations that you cannot fulfill in the process of "making a good impression."

What is the answer? Should you send a written authorization to your psychoanalyst requesting a detailed summary of the findings in your case to your prospective partner? That is obviously not necessary or desirable. To reveal your intimate feelings and key experiences in an honest exchange is not always realistic. Probably the best way is to let the other person know at some early point what the key facts in your life are now—marital status, dependents, preference for or against a firm relationship, occupation, and education. If you are not seeking permanence, these facts may be irrelevant, the key issue being instead whether the two of you will enjoy each other for a while.

It does not make too much sense to say, "Tell me all about yourself" or "How come you never got married?" or "Why did your marriage break up?" Honest answers to these questions might be too complicated to explain spontaneously. It is more sensible to express your feelings and memories as they become relevant. You cannot spend much time with a person without being reminded of all kinds of significant experiences, feelings, and so on. Why not reveal yourself to the other person in doses that can be absorbed.

A serious problem occurs when two people have very dissimilar backgrounds. One example is the person married at an early age for a considerable length of time who then meets somebody who has been single or separated for a considerable time. Many people, widowed or divorced when no longer young, complain about the lack of respect their new acquaintances have for them, or the lack of commitment they have to a stable relationship. The person who went right into marriage after high school, many years ago, and now enters the singles scene will have experiences that were unknown to him or her either as a young person or in the shelter of marriage.

I remarked recently to an older woman who complained that men were not treating her with respect that when you are mugged, or your house is burglarized, or you are insulted by a stranger, there is nothing personal about it. You cannot expect to be totally shielded from rough people. You can try to reduce your feelings of vulnerability and learn how to protect yourself.

Early in a relationship you have to discover the difference between genuine feelings, neurotic responses, and just plain malarkey. What does it mean to be told, "You are the most wonderful woman in the world"? What man is in a position to make this statement? For your own good, accept this kind of talk with a grain of salt—enjoy it but be aware that the other person may use flattery as a weapon.

It is normal to want a certain amount of praise but don't let it cloud your perceptions. One woman reported, "I can't have sex until I have rosy feelings, so I tell myself the other person is completely sincere and pretend to have feelings in response to his." One man habitually says, "You have a greater potential for love than I," feeling that most people want others to bring them out. These little games are quite common. They are harmless and even amusing when two self-assured people play with each other. They both know that they are entertaining and being entertained.

However, when one person is manipulating and the other person is in deadly earnest, the latter risks a great deal of pain. Pretending that a relationship is good is doing a disservice not only to yourself but to the other person, because he or she may be continuing the relationship under the assumption that you are both satisfied. Try to know what your feelings are, express them accurately, and insist that the other person be equally honest.

How to Handle Doubt

Is it wise to withdraw immediately when you see signs of strain or should you test the relationship further? Ideally you should aim for a balance between acceptance of another person's failings and weak spots and an awareness that he or she doesn't have your welfare at heart. People do make honest mistakes; they do try to correct their personalities; they do attempt to adapt to new circumstances. On the other hand, they also lie, exploit, behave sadistically, and mistreat others in various ways.

The central decision has to be based on whether you feel that somebody's life-style and personal goals will be compatible with yours. Do both of you have similar ideas concerning the nature of a relationship, the degree of commitment, and so on? If most signals are "Go," find a reasonable time to say what you want and to discuss any potential problem areas. Try to be matter of fact. If the other person initiates such a discussion, learn how to listen. It is unquestionably painful to be told about somebody else's dissatisfaction with you or the relationship. It can also be discouraging or disappointing. However, you may be learning something very valuable about yourself. You will also discover a good deal about the style of the other person. Is there compassion, sarcasm, encouragement, deep-rooted frustrations or hostilities, dispassionateness or prejudice?

Even what seems to be a reasonable expression of resentment can be a displacement from another situation. By understanding this, you will be able to save the relationship or remove yourself from it without feeling degraded or rejected. Displacement is quite common when somebody has been recently rejected and takes out feelings of rejection on a third party.

Another hazard is emotional timidity. Some people are reluctant to be open until the other person commits himself or herself. This emotional restraint is usually due to past hurts, rejections, low self-esteem, and so on. If you find yourself acting, or not acting, out of this sort of timidity, try to break the pattern because it only increases the likelihood that your feelings will not be reciprocated. The other person has to know them in order to respond. Only then can you know if your intensity is more than the other person can handle, and whether your deep feelings are shared. Whatever the response is, you will have gained essential information.

It is important to remember that an early burst of feelings—love at first sight—may be based on immature fantasies. You should be careful to determine whether you are seeing the other part realistically.

How to Proceed

Assuming that you feel the relationship is worth building on, how do you proceed? When you love someone, you often set up expectations for the other party to fulfill. These may not be realistic, so your first responsibility is to be careful about expecting too much and antagonizing your partner unnecessarily. If you find that your partner is not responding as intensely as you are, though he or she wants to maintain the relationship, take it easy. An imbalance between the feelings of two people is common. The relationship may be good and ought not to be broken. Be emotionally generous and don't expect the world. Only when you see that there is no real reciprocity in the relationship should you consider terminating it.

The key issue is not an exact equality of feelings but rather goodwill, commitment, and shared values and goals.

Experience teaches that when two people want each other,

they can solve the problems between them. When one person does not wish to be committed, no amount of settling differences will have any effect. Nothing is going to happen. In short, without mutual goodwill and determination, there is no real relationship. With it, any strange pair of personalities can mate and love successfully.

Chapter 16

Building Constructive Relationships

I asked a large group, "What is a constructive relationship?" From the richness and variety of their answers you can tell that, even though there is no single definition, people do have specific ideas on the subject. Here are some of the responses:

- One that doesn't raise the issue of dominance.
- One that leaves you feeling good about yourself.
- It involves being sensitive to the other person.
- One in which you feel so comfortable that you can say anything.
- One in which you are forgiving when somebody treads on your sensitivities.
- A mutual exchange, with each person giving something to the relationship.
- When you feel accepted because the other person takes your ugly as well as your good parts.
- One in which you can be critical.
- One with take and give.
- One that's fun.
- A caring relationship.
- One is which both people can and do express concern.
- One in which both people feel comfortable and happy.

• One that encourages growth.

What is generally considered a constructive relationship is an open exchange that does not fear a loss of closeness because of resentment and allows the opportunity to be yourself and grow.

Building Self-understanding

A firm relationship is most likely when both partners are aware of their own personalities. Some self-awareness is necessary in selecting a partner and in stage-managing your life in such a way that your needs are satisfied and your goals are reached.

Develop a clear sense of your own identity. Evaluate yourself as a person. Conceptualize your self-image. What role do you play in life, that is, what is the particular nature of your relationships with the significant people around you? Discover the ways in which you are unique!

Decide what you want from other people. Evaluate your needs and be aware of those that you can reasonably expect your partner to fulfill and which needs you must satisfy yourself. Then, do what you have to do without whining!

Clarify and express your personal and mutual goals. Sharing in its most complete sense requires a pooling of resources in order to develop a compatible style of life. One of your important goals may be somewhat outside the relationship, for example, building a career. Your potential partner's goal may focus on home and family. The goals can be different but complementary.

Build Social Sensitivity

Social sensitivity and self-understanding are part of the same process. The current emphasis upon doing your own thing and, by inference, not taking responsibility for your effects upon others can be followed to dangerous extremes. There is a big difference between throwing off neurotic obligations and behaving responsibly in a relationship. When you have made an emotional commitment to someone, you may safely assume that deep feelings, including resentment and frustration, will sooner or later be stirred up, unless the other person is totally detached. Therefore, a degree of sensitivity to that person's feelings and the part you play in them is necessary.

Become aware of your feelings. By being more sensitive to both pain and joy, you increase the meaning of your relationships. However, it is also important that you develop objectivity. Always remember that feelings can deceive you, so make the effort to match them against the facts. Awareness of the nuances of your emotional life can offer important information as to whether a relationship is constructive or destructive. You can determine whether you are being fed emotionally, growing, or perhaps being hampered or worn down in subtle ways.

Become aware of your partner's feelings. Stop, look, and listen! Overcome egocentricity! Don't be aware only of your own overpowering needs. Become aware of the resentments you create in others. By learning increased sensitivity to the signs of pleasure and resentment in others, you will gain insight into your own qualities, which may be quite different from those you imagine. Be alert to whether the other person wants more or less closeness, freedom, and so on.

Live in the present. Be aware of whether your reactions are appropriate to the present or transferences from the past. Determine whether the other person is meeting your current needs. Do not oppress others with the emotional disasters of your earlier life or expect them to make up the emotional deficits of the past. Learn how to recognize a good moment. Enjoy what you can.

Building Personal Self-esteem

Insist on good treatment. A relationship cannot be constructive if you believe that you are being badly treated. A close relationship can bring out your worst qualities or cause you to feel ashamed of the things you have done. Act responsibly toward the other person and insist on the same for yourself.

Use the "Ouch Principle." Some of you have been trained to excuse yourself when somebody steps on you. Learn to express your hurt.

Learn how to fight back. It isn't true that fighting back will destroy a solid relationship. If a relationship is worth saving, you should fight back to change the undesirable qualities before you become too dissatisfied to want to remedy the situation.

Support the other person's self-esteem. It may seem incongruous to follow a suggestion that you learn how to fight back with the admonition to support the other's self-esteem. Not so. It makes emotional common sense that you cannot have self-respect or emotional fulfillment when you are surrounded by people whom you mistreat. Therefore, to build a relationship, it is vital to acknowledge and bolster the other person's sense of self-respect. By creating a feeling of appreciation and a desire to reciprocate, you enhance mutual appreciation and closeness.

Building Openness

By openness I mean a willingness to express your feelings and attitudes without fear. It may be the key to a good relationship, because dissatisfactions can come into the open and be resolved.

Be truthful. Unless you express your reactions openly, your relationships will certainly deteriorate. You owe it to yourself to establish your own identity by letting your partner know what is on your mind. The other side of the coin holds also: If you do something that you can't talk about, you may jeopardize a valued relationship.

Bring problems into the open. Antagonisms do not disappear. Discussing the stresses brings an opportunity for improvement and can aid your own peace of mind. You will also discover whether the other person will listen to your complaints, is truthful, and can compromise.

Nevertheless, solving problems does not create relationships. It is only the desire to stay together that creates the motivation to solve problems. Without the intention of remaining together, no amount of problem solving will help.

Insist on the truth. Closing your eyes to what is really happening does not avert disaster. Learn how to recognize evasions. When these occur, you can be certain that something is going on that you don't like. Perhaps the other person does not respect you because of doubt that you can handle what he or she has to say.

Listen to the other person's complaints. Even with the best intentions, from time to time you may express unconscious hostilities, be insensitive, make poor judgments or emotional demands, and so on. Get feedback so that you can understand how you have been contributing to the other person's emotional stress.

Don't exaggerate. Sarcasm, temper outbursts, exaggerated expressions of pain and anger, all escalate a bad situation into a worse one. Deal objectively with one issue at a time.

Don't assume. Many of you assume that you understand a loved one's mind. You may also assume that he or she knows your mind. When reproaches develop because of misunderstanding, neglect, and so forth, the misperception is obvious. When you don't know, or are not sure, ask. When you want something, or believe something, speak up.

Know when to give or take "no" for an answer. Mutual respect requires that each person have some veto over what happens in his or her life. There will be occasions, even in good relationships when unreasonable requests are made. Those are the times to say no, or accept the other person's refusal. Nagging is self-destructive because it transforms you and the other person into adversaries. If you are constantly being told "no," then something serious is wrong, either in the relationship or in your demands.

Building Intimacy

Many singles feel obliged to hold back their feelings or are hampered in being expressive. There is a connection between poor relationships and being emotionally hampered. Many aspects of a relationship are damaged when feelings are not expressed. People who cannot express their feelings are more likely to select and maintain poor relationships. A lack of emotional expression and communication causes the deterioration of a relationship, reducing self-confidence, warmth, and optimism. Emotional distance is increased, as well as suspiciousness and/or negative expectations. Barriers to intimacy become greater and ultimately can lead to the dissolution of the strongest relationship.

Learn how to express warmth. Nothing is as important in the creation of good feelings as the open expression of liking, acceptance, and goodwill. Try to recognize deficiencies in this area and take steps to overcome them. A group experience is often helpful.

Learn how to accept warmth. It is astonishing that so many people will believe degrading messages, yet refuse to believe pleasant ones. *Giving* love is important, but it's equally important to be accepting of love. It is an essential part of building a relationship.

Learn how to compromise. Anybody who has gone beyond the stage of fantasy realizes that relationships require some compromise. Respect the other person's legitimate rights. The inability to compromise can show itself through intellectual arrogance and the bullying of the other person into giving you what you want.

Avoid silly fights. Most issues people fight about lack either importance or an objective criterion as to right and wrong. Dominance and superiority are the real issues. You must learn how to keep these out of discussions if you want to have and maintain enjoyable relationships. The real issue in an argument as to whether Beethoven or Mozart is the superior composer might be: "Stop ramming your ideas down my throat."

If there are substantial conflicts in your life about which you cannot compromise, for example, religious faith, children, money, then you may be involved with the wrong person.

Create trust. This implies that in time of trouble you will be available. It is also something that you have a right to expect. I know one marriage that went on the rocks because the husband went out of town on business when his wife underwent a serious operation. When she recovered, she called him and told him he was through. Rightfully so.

Plan together. Working on the future together is the real test of an intimate relationship. If you or the other person cannot take responsibility for planning vacations, housing, and visits to friends, then one of you is displaying a lack of personal identity and placing a vast burden on the other person.

Permit intimacy to happen. It is too easy to create so much activity—scheduled events, music, other people, TV, radio, books—that no significant exchange of feelings occurs. Therefore, if your relationship is so busy that no subtle awareness and no bond of real companionship is expressed, it is possible that your partner or you are deliberately creating a barrier. You might look into your own feelings and discover that you are giving yourself a message of dissatisfaction. If you value intimacy, you must stage-manage your life to make it possible.

Offer your reactions. You cannot expect intimacy from another person unless you are prepared to offer it. It is helpful to express your reactions to the relationship and what is taking place.

Ask questions. Do not guess. If you suspect something significant is going on but are not sure, don't guess. Don't rely on astrological signs; don't trust your intuition. Make sure.

Be accepting. It is futile to expect intimacy when you misuse the information and feelings that are offered you. Accept a different opinion or reaction. Don't "editorialize" or comment on everything because you know better. Sometimes "I understand" or "that's too bad" or "good luck" is all that is needed. Create an atmosphere in which truthfulness is encouraged.

Be revealing. It is reasonable to let the other person know about previous experiences or memories. It puts you in perspective. Since the truth will out, it is perhaps better to tell something about yourself in measured doses rather than create an air of mystery. Buried corpses have a way of surfacing!

Learn how to listen. Stop operating only on your own inner TV. Turn down your own transmitter and turn up your receiver. Intimacy implies that you are sensitive to the other person's feelings.

Building Autonomy

It is not contradictory to conclude a chapter on building a firm relationship with a section on autonomy, or the value of appreciating your personal identity. The best way to ruin a relationship is to demand that it meet all your needs.

Avoid clutching. Give the other person room to breathe. When you act as though only your partner can keep you from being depressed or lonely, you reveal yourself as an inadequate person, unable to stand on your own two feet. Don't prevent the other person from growing or participating in activities that are important to him or her.

Avoid dominance. What you may think is simply a pleasant form of leadership could have a variety of very destructive meanings. Unlearn the model you may have seen at home of one person subjugating the other.

Encourage the other person's development. This shows your goodwill and your maturity. Leave breathing space by permitting separation for schooling, hobbies, career, and so on.

Evaluate your own development. Ask yourself if you are giving too much time and energy to do something for the other person that he or she could do for himself or herself. Do you wait for the other person to do something, even if it is inconvenient, that you could do for yourself? Do you feel like an equal partner, a lord, a servant, or a cripple? Are you growing, doing new things, getting better at the old ones, and comfortable during temporary absences? Are you a separate person who contributes equally to the relationship, or are you in orbit around a superior being, without whom you feel you are nothing?

These guidelines will help maintain fundamentally sound relationships on a firm basis.

Chapter 17

Living Successfully with Yourself

Recently I met a couple who had just celebrated their fiftieth wedding anniversary. They had been reared as brother and sister, their parents having married after the death of their first spouses. Imagine—an entire lifetime spent without worrying whether one is loved or where the next date is coming from!

This kind of long-term relationship is rare. Most of us have to deal with separateness and learn to live successfully with ourselves, which requires personal growth. Many people erroneously believe that only in marriage can they find fulfillment, as the following comments indicate.

"I feel more autonomous when I have a secure marriage. It is a base."

"I can use the security of the relationship to build autonomy. It is a horrible feeling to plummet down with nothing to hold on to."

"I feel like a little child when nobody feeds me. It's an awful mess. If you can feed yourself, you're not hungry."

The above comments to the contrary, many relationships foster dependency and incompetence. Autonomy flourishes in a relationship only when you are strong and independent and encourage the other person to feel the same. It is even more likely when you and the other person are friends, who want success for one another and value each other's uniqueness.

Why Autonomy?

To achieve autonomy is to have the best of two worlds. If fate deprives you of a partner, or provides one who is emotionally distant, you still have the potential to be yourself and enjoy life. If you are with a mature partner, one with a developed inner life and sense of separate identity, you are a better partner by being able to avoid irritating demands. You will also be able to enjoy your partner's personality. Ask yourself the following questions. Do I . . .

• Allow living space for the other person to express his or her individuality?
• Assume a fair share of the burden?
• Develop my own competence?
• Give up too much time and energy to do things for the other person that he or she should or could do independently?
• Wait for the other person to do something, even if it is inconvenient for him or her?
• Like to learn how to do things, be independent, feel like an equal partner, only to find that I end up being told that I am stupid and feeling like a child?

If the other person is extremely passive, you may want to encourage greater participation on his or her part. To involve him or her, you must first relax—let something remain undone. For once say, "I forgot to get tickets, how come you didn't remind me or get them yourself?" If you have worked your way into the role of parent, encourage the other person to grow up. Let go.

The Passive Partner

Should you find yourself comfortably giving in to the inclination to be lazy and letting the other person take charge, remind yourself that free rides don't last forever. Your partner is not going to be content to shoulder the burden indefinitely, and if he or she is, and you feel content in a relationship with such a pushover, a look at your own motives is in order. If you are aware that your own struggle to grow up is being thwarted, let the other person know that you want to be an equal, not an inferior.

In considering the issue of submissiveness and dominance, ask yourself these questions:

- Why do I allow other people to manipulate me?
- Why do I let others make me feel guilty?
- Why do I let people in authority exercise power that exists only in my own mind?
- Why do I accept what is handed to me?

The answer is probably that you were conditioned as a child to do what you were told. When you were weak, vulnerable, and unformed, your parents and other authorities required you to be compliant. You may not have been encouraged to develop your identity. As a result, many of you have never grown up. You still let others exercise unnecessary power over you.

Developing Strength

Learn to experience your personal authority. Discover what is valuable to you; become assertive and act in your own interests. By developing genuine strength, you will neither be pushed around nor will you exploit others. You can develop freedom without anger, hostility, sulking, or self-degradation. Understand and express your own individuality.

Frequently, the issue is not who is more competent but who is the boss. Overly dominant people frequently act bossy because they have been pushed around and seek revenge. Perhaps this is the model they've learned.

It is natural that some differences exist in people's levels of assertiveness. However, substantial differences do put a strain on a relationship, because they may lead to the stifling of initiative and the creation of passivity. Resentment arises concerning a loss of identity, problems of responsibility, an inability to become autonomous, and so on.

If there is question of who is "the boss," some mutual adjustment will help a truly collaborative relationship to develop. Perhaps one person should take the initiative to change. Psychotherapeutic assistance could be considered. Perhaps only a premarital divorce will help.

Living successfully with yourself creates the opportunity for an emotionally fulfilled life. A survey of yourself in these areas can serve to motivate you toward active steps to improve your life. Think of maturity as having fulfilled yourself to a great extent in many of the following areas:

- The capacity for deep emotional experience
- A sense of purposeful striving and direction
- Self-understanding
- Acceptance of others
- Self-acceptance
- Ability to form relationships
- A sense of having overcome difficulties through struggle
- Autonomy, or the ability to stand on one's own feet emotionally and intellectually

Guide for Action

Here are some practical suggestions for reducing inadequacies and developing an autonomous attitude toward life:

Recognize the importance of autonomy. To live successfully with yourself you must:

Reject totally the idea that self-sufficiency is impossible or means social isolation.

Resist social pressure to conform, to participate in others' activities that you dislike.

Learn how to reject others' unfair criticism.

When I start to work on this area with my patients, I sometimes invite them to go to the window of my office and shout to
the world: "Your opinions mean nothing to me." Even though *I*
pay the rent there, they generally don't dare express their independence. Only one man, sixty-seven years old, sick of therapy
after over thirty years (mostly with someone else), finally
screamed his defiance!

Clarify your identity. The word "autonomy" derives from
"self." New activities to improve your life will be most fulfilling
when they are consistent with your vital qualities.

How to do this?

Who are you? R. N. Bolles, in *What Color Is Your Parachute,*
suggests that you might answer the question "Who am I?" ten
to fifteen times. After each response write, "This turns me on
because . . ." or "This turns me off because . . ." Clarifying
your picture of yourself can lead to a more independent life-
style. Self-understanding is a guide for eliminating self-destructiveness and enhancing constructive action.

Self-inventory

YOUR BODY
    Make a realistic appraisal of yourself in the areas of
    Energy level and stamina
    Health

YOUR TEMPERAMENT
    Typical moods (pleasant, unpleasant, unpredictable)
    Sensitivity and openness to the world or closed off
    Courage or fearfulness
    Preference for security or preference for excitement
    Preference for stability or preference for variety
    Preference for working toward goals or preference for plea-
    sure/play
    Preference for organized situations or preference for unstruc-
    tured situations

YOUR VALUES

List the three ideals that are most important to you—the situations and activities that are most rewarding.

Now list the three activities or philosophical ideas that are most repugnant to you—the negative values you find it important to avoid.

Finally, list any areas in which you are in conflict, that is, about which you are emotionally torn because actions to which you are drawn also have a negative value.

YOUR GOALS

List three personal goals.

What is your professional goal?

Are your goals realistic?

Are your standards of success too high or too low?

Do you have the capability to reach these goals?

Are you ready to invest time, money, and so on to reach your goals?

Do your values lead toward these goals or are they in conflict?

Are they your goals or has somebody selected them for you?

YOUR IDENTITY

Identify and eliminate the self-hating parts of your identity. Stop treating yourself with cruelty.

Reject the burden of neurotic criticism bestowed on you by others, which you let flourish in the moist, dank recesses of your soul.

Live constructively, think positively, and build a genuine self-esteem through a warm interest in the welfare of others.

Do not let people degrade you.

Take a few risks in order to exchange good experience and self-acceptance for the garbage you have accumulated to date.

YOUR MOTIVATIONS TO CHANGE

Recognize signs of stress. Motivate yourself to make constructive changes. Ask yourself if you are subject to:

Depression

Bodily symptoms, i.e., diarrhea, sleeplessness, fatigue, sweating

Anxiety and fear

Guilt

Tension and conflicts

Anger and fits of rage

Irritability

Feeling emotionally deprived

Feeling rejected, humiliated, or hurt

Job dissatisfaction

Low self-esteem

Unpleasant fantasies, bad dreams, nightmares

Inability to sleep

Feeling apathetic, hopeless, helpless

Feeling socially detached, withdrawn, not belonging

YOUR SOCIAL LIFE

Friendship has much in common with frankly sexual attachments. Warmth or coldness, acceptance or hostility, intimacy or distance, commitment or detachment, can occur in both. Friendship is an important part of emotional fulfillment, acts as a source of joy in good times and solace in bad ones. There are vital reasons why your capacity to develop it should be enhanced.

Here is how some people experience the problem of making and keeping friends:

• I want to make friends.

• I need more continuous friendships.

• I need more friends, because I only see my girl during the weekend.

• I limit my relationships to business. I want to create more personal relationships.

• I have no relatives. I live alone and need an opportunity to meet and interact with people in a worthwhile activity.

• I have difficulty in meeting people.

• I want to relate to all kinds of people, especially the difficult types.

Forming varied and close friendships is actually an excellent form of expressing your autonomy, insofar as it removes you from excessive dependency upon a mate.

Fight reliance on a limited number of friends. You must realize that one person cannot meet your needs totally. Avoid being a clutcher. Find one friend to play bridge with, another to go to concerts with, and so on. Of course, do not let clutchers get a firm hold on you. There is no point in working toward freedom while you are carrying the burden of a too-dependent friend or partner. Be firm. Do not sacrifice yourself unnecessarily. Besides, it is no kindness to keep somebody else from enjoying the rarefied atmosphere of autonomous heights.

Some people have special difficulty in achieving autonomy because they have a reverse dependency: They need to be needed. Superficially, it seems that they are independent and strong. In actuality, they only feel valuable if there is another person who tells them they are important. Therefore, they are as dependent as the other person, even though they don't experience themselves this way. This is a trap to be avoided if you wish to experience emotional freedom.

YOUR LIKES

Tally what gives you pleasure. Make a list of all the things you like to do. It should include fun and games at all stages of your life. Give yourself time to take up hobbies and other activities you have had a yearning to resume.

YOUR NEW ACTIVITIES

Invite new experiences. Many of you may have seen pianist Arthur Rubinstein on TV in late 1977. His career had just been prematurely (at the age of ninety) terminated by visual problems. What was his reaction? Despair? Drugs? Alcohol? No, he started to listen to new music that he had not previously heard because he was too busy playing. He described the arguments he had in his mind with the performers because he didn't always approve of their approach. The moral is this: Even at the age of ninety you can enjoy new and joyful experiences if you have a positive attitude toward life. You can fight despair. There are new joys to be discovered. Try to develop friendships with people who will take you on new, unfamiliar pathways. Some activities encourage travel. Concentration on one interest develops your appreciation and understanding in depth. Meaning, anticipation of learning, and new experiences will follow.

YOUR BALANCE BETWEEN AUTONOMY AND RELATEDNESS

Develop interests that integrate private pleasures with social exchanges. My own great love is flower photography. Now, it is true that there can be only one eye behind the viewfinder of a camera. Moreover, when I seek out this pleasure I don't want to be bothered entertaining anybody else. However, I am egotistical enough to want to show my slides to people (in fact, I have sold some for record jackets). Therefore, after a preliminary selection, I screen them for people and invite their comments. Eventually, I end up with a carefully selected portfolio and a group of friends who feel that I am a creative genius (or so I tell myself). In short, some activities can balance both your needs for relatedness as well as for autonomy.

YOUR SCHEDULE

Plan a weekly schedule. You may not be a self-starter. You may need some kind of direction. Learn to give it to yourself. If you wait around for something to happen, it may not. Either you will continue to waste your time in trivial ways, or you will end up by doing what somebody else wants you to do. Locate a list of available activities. If no local list exists, contact all the organizations providing interesting activites and publish your own newsletter. You will make all kinds of contacts and find fun things to do as well.

Get into the habit of planning your activities—in part at least—one week in advance. Keep a calendar noting what you plan to do, including maintaining your home. Then, unless there is a very good reason, follow your schedule. Don't let others interfere with it. If people want to be with you, let them come along, if it is the kind of activity that benefits from company.

The name of this game is self-direction to achieve autonomy. Making unsatisfactory changes in your schedule merely to avoid loneliness is self-destructive to this goal and requires that you return to page 1. No, don't try to return the book to the bookseller, by now it is shopworn.

YOUR LIFE-STYLE

Your life-style is to your actions as your signature is to your handwriting. It is your unique way of being in the world.

If you are like most people, much of your life has developed helter-skelter. You have probably adjusted to circumstances and have not determined where you want to go and how you should improve matters *now*.

Important areas of your life-style include:

Love and intimacy. Most people crave these but let anxiety and participation in self-destructive relationships interfere.

Friendship. Comradeship and companionship add strength, joy, and opportunities for relaxation.

Employment/productivity. For many people life is not complete without doing something that is useful or important to others.

Autonomy/creativity. Develop the capacity to enjoy your own personality. Remember, when you feed yourself emotionally, you lose dependence on others, and paradoxically can form better relationships.

PLEDGE FOR ACTION

Work on your motivation. Decide to eliminate the clinging, incompetent, self-condemning qualities that hamper your freedom.

Develop priorities. Consider your daily activities and decide which are important and which trivial. Relentlessly eliminate those that don't lead toward important goals.

Overcome self-indulgence. This is the chief source of destructive behavior.

Decide what you will do about:
• Self-destructive relationships, actions, attitudes, and health habits
• Developing new cultural and educational experiences
• Working on self-affirmation
• Reaching out to others
• Insisting on your rights and meeting your needs
• Deciding to be a winner

Set up an action schedule to:
• Work on goals
• Work on priorities
• Decide when action must be taken
• Determine when your resources will be ready
• Follow through to make sure others do their share

Postscript

Beethoven Never Changed a Diaper

Until recently, single people have been at the mercy of the marrieds. Religious and civil laws and customs placed them at a disadvantage. In the United States, for example, singles pay disproportionate taxes to support children, spouses, dependent parents, and mortgages of a dominating majority. The number and proportions of singles (including never married, divorced, and widowed) have dramatically increased because of social changes and an increased life span.

To some extent, more and more people are recognizing the advantages of singleness for particular stages of their lives and denying both the sanctity and emotional value of marriage as we have understood it.

One of the greatest misconceptions is that, in contrast to married people, singles are immature and inadequate. Everybody is born dependent, vulnerable, and incompetent. Some people continue through life in fear of losing parental support or of being abandoned. Fear of independence is the basis for the neurosis that afflicts tens of millions in this country.

A more realistic training of children would allow them to learn that relatedness and autonomy alternate, as required by circumstances. Children should be taught to appreciate their own company and be able to entertain themselves without others' presence or encouragement.

Some people who experience inadequacy seek a spouse to provide support and emotional stability. Countless marriages can be equated with neurotic acting-out rather than maturity. Many married people, male and female, demonstrate infantile dependency states. They are unable to function in any kind of independent way, always requiring the presence and support of their spouses. This becomes particularly apparent when a marriage is unexpectedly severed through separation or death. Such people can flounder miserably for years, unable to find new forms of emotional gratification. They need somebody to clutch.

In contrast, the singles who lead worthwhile lives have demonstrated their ability to live independent, mature existences. They have overcome the infantile fantasy that parents will always be there to take care of them. The mature single stands on his or her own two feet, and if marriage is contemplated as an emotionally fulfilling improvement in his or her life, he or she chooses a mate.

Today, men and women can survive separately. No longer do economic, social, and religious conditions enforce cruel, implacable bonds. Now you can ask whether a new relationship will improve your life and act on the basis of your needs.

Mature, autonomous single people see life as a varied experience with many possibilities, contribute to others' welfare without making emotional demands, are self-reliant, and offer as much to a relationship as they take from it.

Some of the greatest people in history, who have contributed most to others' lives:

—Never changed a diaper
—Never attended a P.T.A. meeting
—Never cursed a divorce lawyer

Who are they? Beethoven, Brahms, Schubert, Tchaikovsky. Also Emily Dickinson, Charlotte and Emily Bronte, Jane Austen.

Singles! Raise your heads. You have nothing to lose but your inferiority complex.

Index